JOHN FEE was one of Edinburgh's most accomplished and popular storytellers. Part of a well-known an Irish family, John was born and brought up in the Old Town. His early experiences of the social life and character of Old Edinburgh combined with his later passions for history, art and story to fashion a mature storytelling artist whose dry wit, melodic tenor voice, and cunning digressions kept audiences enthralled. In the last two years of his life John Fee produced written versions of his developed stories for the first time. They comprise an original and revealing insight into real lives, lived in the ancient heart of Scotland's capital city.

STUART MCHARDY is a writer, occasional broadcaster, and storyteller. Having been actively involved in many aspects of Scottish culture throughout his adult life – music, poetry, language, history, folklore – he has been resident in Edinburgh for over a quarter of a century. Although he has held some illustrious positions including Director of the Scots Language Resource Centre in Perth and President of the Pictish Arts Society, McHardy is probably proudest of having been a member of the Vigil for a Scottish Parliament. Often to be found in the bookshops, libraries and tea-rooms of Edinburgh, he lives near the city centre with the lovely (and ever-tolerant) Sandra and they have one son, Roderick.

DONALD SMITH is the Director of Scottish International Storytelling Festival at Edinburgh's Netherbow and a founder of the National Theatre of Scotland. For many years he was responsible for the programme of the Netherbow Theatre, producing, directing, adapting and writing professional theatre and community dramas, as well as a stream of literature and storytelling events. He has published both poetry and prose and is a founding member of Edinburgh's Guid Crack Club. He also arranges story walks around Arthur's Seat.

Edinburgh Old Town

Journeys and Evocations

Exploring the History and Folklore
of Edinburgh's Ancient Heart

JOHN FEE

Accompanied by Stuart McHardy and Donald Smith

Luath Press Limited
EDINBURGH
www.luath.co.uk

First published 2014

ISBN: 978-1-910021-56-9

 Seeing
Stories

The paper used in this book is recyclable.
It is made from low-chlorine pulps
produced in a low-energy, low-emissions
manner from renewable forests.

Printed and bound by
Charlesworth Press, Wakefield

Map by Jim Lewis

Photographs by Stuart McHardy

Typeset in 10.5pt Sabon by
3btype.com

Contents

Acknowledgements

The Scottish Storytelling Forum wishes to acknowledge the friendship and support of John Fee (1930–2011) and his wife Mona Fee. This publication has also been made possible by the enthusiasm and helpfulness of John's daughters Angie and Lorna, and of his many friends and admirers amongst Scotland's storytelling community, not least in Edinburgh.

The Forum is also grateful to the European 'Seeing Stories' landscape narrative project for its assistance in the preparation of this Storyguide to Edinburgh's Old Town. 'Seeing Stories' is supported by the EU Cultural Programme, funded by the European Commission. The content of this book, however, reflects only the views of its author and editors, and the information and its use are not the responsibility of the European Commission or any other cited source, but of the Scottish Storytelling Forum.

Introduction

John Fee was born and brought up in Edinburgh's Old Town, a fourth generation descendant of Irish immigrants. The Fees were part of what was sometimes called 'Little Ireland' in the Cowgate and Grassmarket. But John himself grew up delighting in every aspect of the Old Town community around him. In later life he became devoted to the history of the area, and its part in the wider history of Scotland, Britain and Europe. Through his storytelling, John unified all of his life experiences with his desire to pass on something of value to succeeding generations.

John Fee never spoke casually. His style of speech was considered, sometimes oblique or ironic, occasionally enigmatic. After training as a teacher in later life, John began to give talks on his favourite topic – the Old Town – but these increasingly became virtuoso performances. He was a true storytelling artist, painting verbal pictures, setting off on digressions that turned out not to be digressions, moving effortlessly into a song or poem. John regarded all of these things as part of his inheritance – the culture of the Old Town. To listen to John was to be accepted as part of his community, and magically entertained with a seasoning of education along the way! It was all in his mind and imagination, and only during the last year of his life that John actually wrote down some of the stories which he had crafted as spoken performances.

This volume of the 'Journeys and Evocations' series grows out of John Fee's take on Edinburgh's Old Town, an insider's view, albeit one steeped in accumulated history and lore. It is humane, original, quirky at points, but always wending towards the heart of the matter, and especially told for us the listeners and readers. John's versions of well-known stories always throw fresh light on the matter, but he has also uncovered little-known aspects of the Royal Mile along with long-forgotten characters who spring back to life through the storyteller's art.

We are delighted to present this storytelling experience, walking alongside John, as our tribute to a great urban storyteller and fine human being, truly 'a man you don't meet every day'.

STUART MCHARDY and DONALD SMITH

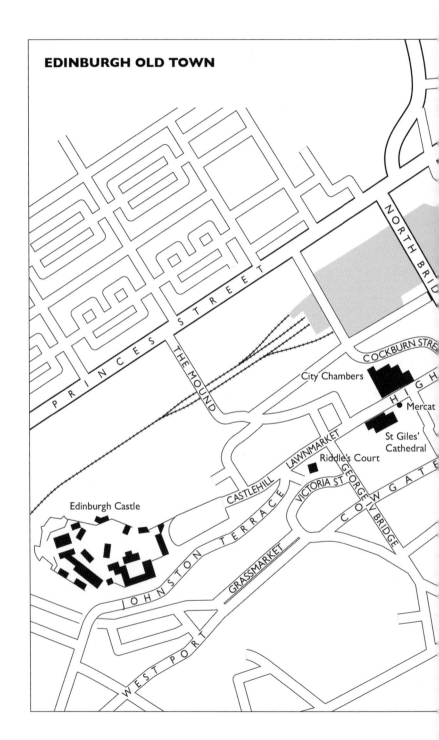

EDINBURGH OLD TOWN

PRINCES STREET

THE MOUND

NORTH BRIDGE

COCKBURN STREET

City Chambers

HIGH

Mercat

St Giles' Cathedral

LAWNMARKET

Riddle's Court

CASTLEHILL

VICTORIA ST

GEORGE IV BRIDGE

COWGATE

Edinburgh Castle

JOHNSTON TERRACE

GRASSMARKET

WEST PORT

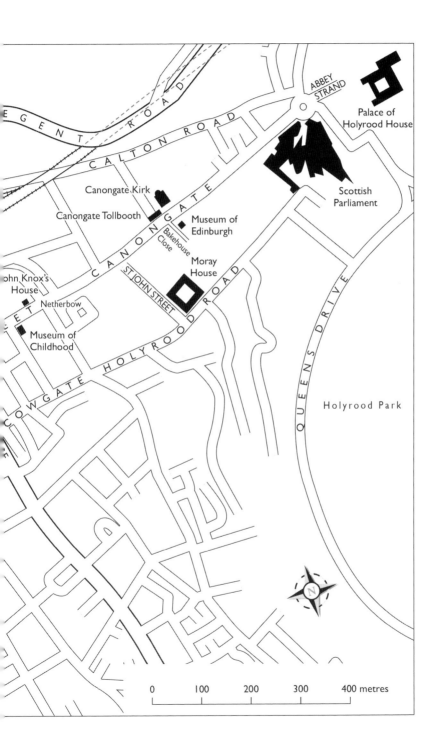

ABBEY STRAND

Palace of
Holyrood House

CALTON ROAD

REGENT ROAD

Canongate Kirk

Canongate Tollbooth

CANONGATE

Museum of
Edinburgh

Bakehouse
Close

Moray
House

Scottish
Parliament

John Knox's
House

Netherbow

Museum of
Childhood

ST JOHN STREET

HOLYROOD ROAD

COWGATE

HOLYROOD

QUEENS DRIVE

Holyrood Park

N

| 0 | 100 | 200 | 300 | 400 metres |

An Old Town Journey

It was one of those Edinburgh mornings when you wake up thinking you have arrived in heaven. The sun was climbing languorously in the east throwing every contour and shadow of the Old Town into bright relief. But as I came through the narrow shaded passage of Castlehill, light flooded across the Castle esplanade illuminating landscape and sky with surreal clarity.

I was the last to arrive. Stuart McHardy was already set up with a big camera, like some latter day Octavius Hill, catching the urban panorama with its early morning face. But John Fee was on the south side gazing down into the Grassmarket. He was, as ever, impeccably turned out with a smart jacket and pork pie hat precisely tilted over his luminous spectacles and prominent nose. Three storytellers, but we all knew whose ear was closest to the whispers and the heartbeats of this special place.

'I was born down there, Donald,' John mused almost to himself, 'I was born within earshot of gunfire; I suppose you could call it "friendly gunfire". Just brought into the world, one of the first sounds I must have heard was the firing of a gun, and from then on once a day, six days a week except Christmas Day and Good Friday and of course, the war years. When the clock struck one, off went the gun – bang on time! And it was loud too, for the window of the kitchen I was born in looked directly on to the castle from where the gun was fired, and is still fired today.'

'What about the bagpipes, John?'

'The sound of the pipes – the silver chanter – and drums! No mere show piece, Edinburgh Castle, as a garrison. Regiments came and went, each one in turn to do guard duties and beat the retreat on the esplanade at the going down of the sun on summer evenings. No big crowds, no scaffolded tiers of seats, no film cameras or floodlights then. Children playing their games in that street below the castle would

stop at the first skirl of the pipes and climb up those steep flights of
steps two at a time, from the Castle Wynd to the Castle Hill where
a small group of spectators would be standing to watch that time-
honoured custom – the beating of the retreat by the resident regiment's
pipe band. Up and down they would march, pipers and drummers for
at least 20 minutes. Is it any wonder then that a small Grassmarket
boy's ambition might be to become a piper or a drummer? But when
I reached the ripe old age of 20, I had become neither a piper nor
drummer.

'Then it happened; I received the invitation to join Her Majesty's Forces
– an offer that could not be refused – and that is how I found myself far
north in that Alcatraz of a place, Fort George, the training depot for all
Highland regiments as a reinforcement for my father's old regiment, the
Argyll and Sutherland Highlanders. And the training in Fort George –
but of that enough said! Yet there was one consolation – immediately
after reveille, the pipes and drums gave out with "Hey Johnnie Cope"
and late, just after lights out, a lone piper played "Fingal's Weeping".
I say this was a consolation, Donald, because it reminded me of home
beneath the castle where I was just longing to be.'

'What happened to all those old soldiers, John?' Stuart had wandered
over to join us. 'Did they come back here to the castle?'

'Aye well, this was their home, Stuart, their home,' and John's gaze
turned towards the climbing battlements.

Old Soldiers

Few folk got to sleep early on the night of 11 November 1918 in the
wide street below that towering rock with an ancient castle perched
upon it – the Grassmarket. It was, of course, the same on that night for

those living in any of Edinburgh's Old Town streets, not just in the Grassmarket. Yet, how often had that street, in centuries past, been a 'no man's land' between the guns of that castle and those of its besiegers. It seemed somehow historically fitting that a great rejoicing should be going on there as neighbours celebrated the end of a war that was meant to end all wars.

It had all begun in earnest just after tea-time, and now there was smoke and fire everywhere, more in fact than on a similar cold winter's night two years previously when a German Zeppelin bombed that very street. But this time there were fireworks, bells ringing, pipes playing and people singing. Even the loud crackle of an enormous bonfire in the centre of the street found it hard to be heard, its leaping flames of orange and yellow framed in every shop window. There were not, however, many uniformed figures among those dancing around it. Scottish losses in the war that ended that day were to total nearly one-fifth of British dead. Yet there were ways that the First World War was not to be quite over for some time to come. It was there to be 'tasted' by Grassmarket children still to be born. For youngsters in the '30s there was still plenty of it around the neighbourhood; indeed, without reference to it many social aspects of their conscious environment would have been inexplicable, would not have made sense.

It was why old Dowd's right arm ended in a steel hook; why old Dawson was stone deaf; and why old Currie shook his head so violently at times. It was why someone's Dad could only sleep when his head was under the blanket, but then would suddenly waken with a great yell, his eyes closed, and this especially during after-dinner naps. But his family just laughed – not at him, but at the sudden start it would give an unknown visitor there in the kitchen which was also his bedroom and also served as the sitting room. If shellshock was only half-understood by Grassmarket youngsters, it was never really understood by the military until well on in that war and even then not fully.

From time to time there would be an evening, usually on a Friday or Saturday, when a group of these war survivors could be found in one of their homes, usually in the kitchen. It would be after pub closing time, and there would never be more than four or five of them; some of them related to each other in kinship, obviously all of them through 'drink': mostly working men in their 40s or 50s, maybe older or younger. But a stronger bond existed for these 'Old Contemptibles' in that they were all survivors of the so-called Great War. The Kaiser referred to the first British troops to land in France as a 'contemptible little army' and the name stuck.

To the children of that house, listening in to these sessions before being packed off to bed, and listening after that, it did seem that for these old warriors their war had been a 'great' war indeed; a subject they were likely to go on and on about. Maybe that was why the woman of the house, once she saw that the guests were suitably welcomed – five 'screw-top' bottles of beer from the cupboard under the sink placed on the table – now disappeared to her sister's house next door. But though she often sighed that it was a man's world – she liked these men, two of whom were her brothers. She might herself get caught up in all this reminiscence when later she would go back to the kitchen to lay out the plate with bread and strong cheese, someone asking her for confirmation of some past occurrence or for a name long forgotten. Otherwise she left them to it.

So the old soldiers went on with what at times came close to being an unashamed glorification of war, though to young unseen listeners who had been packed off to bed, it seemed ages before they got to anything exciting at all. More likely it was all about the squeezing to death between their forefingers and thumbs of countless lice they plucked from the wet pleats of their kilts as they crouched in flooded trenches through days and nights; or twisting and turning, trying to keep warm. Playing at 'sodjers' was far more exciting than that. Nobody in that kitchen seemed to have done anything heroic at all. It must have been a boring war.

Then the pictures on the wall began to play a part. As the old warriors sat around that kitchen table, the only time they took their eyes off each other, or the beer, was when a head was nodded or a finger pointed at a picture. It might be a picture of one who was no longer with them. 'Aye, he wis hame on leave a' right, but when he went back it wis jist tae git himself killed. She hudnae been playing the game an' he kent it!'

At another picture on the same wall: 'And that laddie! That laddie died in ma airms.' Then an old faded postcard-sized picture was fumbled amidst others from an inside pocket, like the kind one might see in bundles in a junk shop window, and held up for inspection.

'Dae ye mind him? He wis nae coward that yin. He came through Passchendaele, didn't he? Three British soldiers killed for every two Germans. Three for every officer. He didnae hear any whistle tae go over the top because he didnae hear any bloody thing – didnae ken where he bloody wis! They shot 'im aw the same.' He was speaking of his brother. Balding and greying heads nodding, and grim 'ayes' were the only acknowledgements given by his companions around that table.

The songs they sang were, of course, all about the subject they had been discussing: 'Roses in Picardy', 'Keep the Homefires Burning', but also songs that came straight to the point – for them that is. So it was, 'Ah

Want tae Go Home'. Then a song with a rousing chorus that began with this:

> Come listen and ah'll I tell ye, how the Jocks spent last New Year.
> Sittin' in the God-damn trenches wi' mud right up tae here.
> They were soaking through. They were soaking through.

So they went on, between sips of beer, one song after another. If it did not all quite add up to a glorification of war, it did tend to suggest a jollification of one – they were having fun singing these war songs; songs that recalled a shared experience that must have meant something to them after all that time.

In ethical terms it seemed to have nothing to do with good or bad. There was no talk of good or bad Germans, or the best ones being dead ones – not in that gathering. There was a war to be won and the enemy was 'Jerry'; so it was a case of 'Jerry' moved here or 'Jerry' moved there. Sometimes the kitchen table became the 'field of action' – beer mugs or forefingers traced out frontline trenches or movements that rarely varied. Apart from patrols, it was either 'pulling back,' 'heads down', or 'over the top'. But these old soldiers were not playing war games. They were not distinguished generals of previous wars recalling how their battles were fought and won. Most of the tracing on the kitchen table was simply to indicate the places where, for comrades in arms, friends, and relatives, that war had ended with shell or machine gun fire, a sniper's bullet, or drowning in the mud. Yet there was no lamenting or shaking of heads as names were reeled off. It was all recalled grimly enough but in a matter-of-fact way.

Well, of course, it all came to an end just like the Great War did and it finished with a song, a song that one might have expected would have set them all apart again – a challenge to any regimental diehard, yet they actually requested it for, after all, their host was an old Argyle, and he sang it:

> Ye may talk aboot yer Gordons an' yer gallant Forty-Twa, Yer silver streakit Seaforths an' yer Camerons sae braw,
> But gie tae me the tartan o' the lads that look sae fine,
> The Argyle and Sutherland Highlanders – The Thin Red Line!

A stirring song it was and the company joined in the rollicking 'Too-ra-loo-ra' chorus after each verse. Then they went off. All that talking, banter, and singing – swirling smoke testing the lungs of those who had survived the mustard gas of the Western Front.

But now the woman of the house had arrived – she had timed it well. She could be made out vaguely through the haze of strong tobacco pipe smoke that filled that small enough kitchen. Great thick white clouds changed to a yellow mist as they swirled around the hissing gas mantle, moving across the pictures on the walls that could hardly be seen. Pictures that had served their purpose that night as entries to the labyrinths of memories shared.

The wee ones, rubbing their eyes, were shooed back to bed from concealed and not-so-concealed 'observation posts', clutching pennies they had fully expected, for these old men of war were among those visitors who always had something to give the bairns. As for the bairns, well, it had been worthwhile keeping awake; better than those nights which were all about politics and trade unions, when nothing listened into could be understood. Besides, some had had a good giggle and the older ones had caught the drift of a story or two. But the war was over for them too – until the next time. The woman of the house was back in command. Shaking her head as she cleared the table, she might well have reflected on the words of a song that would not have been missed out that night:

Old soldiers never die, never die, never die.
Old soldiers never die, they only fade away.

Nevertheless, our old soldiers did die, but not before what they were always gravely predicting came true. The Grassmarket went to war again and young soldiers, sailors and airmen, went off to fight in another world war. Even the lassies who were never allowed to play at 'sodjers' went off too. Soon there were new souvenirs for children to collect and swap: fragments of shot-down enemy aircraft this time, and more service cap badges than during the previous war. Old soldiers were not to be entirely left out of the action either – 'Dad's Army' was waiting for them. But then the time came when they began to disappear until they had all gone – old soldiers dying, but not quite fading away. Not if they were remembered; and they were – they still are. These old soldiers.

By the time John had finished these recollections of two World Wars, we had wandered down Castlehill to the Ensign Ewart, a regular haunt at one time of the veterans who lived in Old Town tenements in such numbers. Diverting a little along Castle Terrace, we could see the massed chimneys of the Grassmarket.

'There's Auld Reikie,' commented Stuart, camera raised, 'the one-time big smoke.'

'Aye, "lang may your lum reek!" That was a blessing when many knew what real poverty could be like, and the fear of it was always there for themselves and for others,' John rejoined.

I knew how much time and effort John spent helping others on the quiet, and realised as he spoke, where those values had been formed.

'To lack this or that was bad enough, but to be without a fire in the grate on a cold night whatever it was burning – coal, wood, even old shoes – was to be poor indeed. On such a night a neighbour with no smoke rising from his lum was a neighbour in trouble. A no-smoke signal was a silent signal for help, for the poor could be proud. It was a signal then that seldom went unheeded.'

'Must have smogged up the views though,' I thought, looking over to the Art College, 'all those chimneys.' John seemed to read my mind.

'Auld Reekie got reekier and reekier up to the early 1950s when smokeless zones began. Until then on a clear and windless autumn or winter's day, there was that great dark grey cloud of smoke hovering ∿ above the capital. All those thousands of coal fires crackling cheerily in the small ranges and grates. Fires to drive the winter's damp away and dry the washing that hung like pennants and banners from kitchen pulleys.

'The same fires boiled water in those huge black iron pots edging out from the hob to catch the flames – water for the washing. Those black pots boiled the tatties, the ham bones and the tripe. As black as the pot and just as heavy was the huge iron kettle on the hob, its water always near boiling point for the tea that was sure to be offered to someone or other in the course of the day or evening. And even when the gas cooker arrived – also black – well the fire still had to be there since running short of a shilling or a penny for the gas was not uncommon. Anyway gas was not to be wasted, not even waste itself was to be wasted! A great sieve full of wet tea leaves and vegetable peelings was emptied at the back of the fire and, with a shovel, they were dragged forward over the burning coals – a dome-like steaming roof and soon a red-hot one – increasing the heat, making the fire last longer, saving the coal!'

'What about Robert Louis Stevenson, John, and his pictures in the fire?' I asked, thinking that John himself was no mean hand at painting a verbal picture.

'Ah, Donald, that was the thing. The fire with its feasts of pictures – coloured pictures, live pictures, but silent pictures save for the odd puff, hiss or crackle. Pictures forming in those flickering kaleidoscopes of flame that danced before their widening eyes. Flames of every shape and size. Flames of every colour and shade that ever graced a painter's palette. Red leapt into yellow and became orange, then into blue and purple, each colour spinning countless shades of contrast and harmony that formed those ephemeral pictures – mountains, skies, trees and rivers – one moment there, then gone forever. A burning coal trailing a tail of black ash would fall into the heart of that friendly inferno, dramatically changing everyone's picture. And now the fire would tire or rather be allowed to tire. It had done its job for young dreamers. Their cocoa cups drained, they had also tired, with the eyes of the youngest almost closed. Whatever the feeble protest, it was time for bed and maybe dreams of ships at sea, or castles in the air.'

'Like that one, then,' added Stuart, looking up towards the looming, slightly ominous ramparts shadowed above us.

'Might be, lads, might be. Time for a story,' says John. 'Shall we bring on the Mountebanks?'

Where were we off to now?

The Mountebanks

The harsh grind of daily life being what it was for most people in earlier times, now and again some sort of cheerful diversion was welcomed. And there were always those willing to provide in some form or another. They were our early buskers, street performers of humble, even despised, status who used their varying talents. Among them were the jugglers, street chanters or singers, dancers, musicians, tumblers or acrobats, storytellers and strolling players.

However welcomed they were by the common folk of the towns and burghs, buskers did not always win the approval of the authorities who regarded them as vagabonds, idlers and beggars – including the fortune-telling gypsies. One of James VI's parliaments sitting in Edinburgh ordered them to be treated as the worst offenders: 'that strolling crew of Egyptians or gypsies who commonly go with blackened faces and speak a foreign language'.

But the dark-skinned, travelling Romany gypsies were not the only outsiders to grace our Old Town streets in the 17th century. Old burgh records and individual diaries suggest that our street entertainment was receiving a lively injection of foreign talent. Names with an international ring appear, like those of artists and performers who appear annually at Edinburgh's International Festival today and have done so since it began. No doubt, entertainers from foreign shores had been making their way to our islands before the 17th century, but it is from that century we begin to hear about them. Performers such as Ponthus, Sarre and Baptista Quaranto became the big stars of our street stages. Even so, as with entertainers in any age, these talented foreigners were not able to please everyone. And among the disgruntled were Edinburgh's physicians who classed all the street artists as 'mountebanks', by which they meant quacks – fake doctors who were resented and despised as rivals for fee-paying patients.

The physicians did of course have a point. The mountebanks' spectacular brand of street performance carried a high-risk factor which drew large crowds. It was to that audience the mountebanks sold their oils, powders and potions, which were far cheaper and which they claimed were more effective than anything the doctors and physicians could prescribe. This was the message preached to the crowds that gathered for the shows. A John Lamont describes one street entertainer in the diary he kept from 1649:

> John Ponthus, the mountebank and jester was now [for] the third time in Scotland. Every time he came he had a public stage erected and sold his drugs and medicines to the people. Each time he had his servants

that danced on the stage leaping and playing the fool, another rope-walking, another fire-eating.

Now, John Ponthus was licensed to set up his makeshift stage at the Mercat Cross in the High Street, or further down in the area between Niddy's Wynd and the top of Blackfriars Street where he could perform and sell his medicines. Diarist John Nicol records that his medicines 'proved very good and real'. Just after Ponthus, John Baptista Quarento – also by kings's warrant and council licence – set up his stage in the same venue for a period of six weeks.

By 1681, the city had its Royal College of Physicians, which was insisting that all medical practitioners be licensed. This was the opposition that Cornelius Tilbourne, the German mountebank, had to face when only about two years later he paid his visit to the capital. This popular performer however had not only a king's warrant but he also wore a medal and chain presented to him in London by the 'merry monarch' himself, Charles II, who had been impressed by a royal performance given at his request by the German. And it is not hard to imagine Cornelius, watched closely by the intrigued king and his courtiers, swallow a deadly poison made and administered to him by top London physicians. Of course he collapsed but was able to swallow his own antidote given quickly to him by his assistant. The daring mountebank then rose to his feet and with great panache acknowledged the resounding applause from his distinguished audience.

Now on an Edinburgh street stage he was, by popular request, about to repeat his London performance, thereby demonstrating the power of his antidote – which would be up for sale – against whatever poison the top Edinburgh physicians had to offer. But this time it was his assistant's turn to swallow the poison, which he did, and as was expected he collapsed before he was given the antidote. Perhaps

Edinburgh's poisons were more potent than London's for the poor fellow promptly died. So that was the end of a bold street entertainer, but it was not, as one might have thought, the end of the mountebanks in Edinburgh. They kept coming.

This was when Sarre the mountebank arrived with his troupe and was granted a licence to erect his stage near Blackfriars Wynd, attracting the customary large crowds and the usual complaints to the council. But this time was worse – the physicians alleged that his cures were making people ill, while wealthy tradesmen objected that the performances were distracting servants from their duties and apprentices from their allotted tasks. So said the master craftsmen.

So Sarre was ordered to dismantle his stage in Blackfriars Wynd, and assigned to perform in a 'more remote' place – the Grassmarket. Perhaps it was felt that folk there were more expendable, or had strong constitutions less likely to succumb to the mountebank's dubious cures. Who knows. As for Sarre, like all the mountebanks, he was a businessman, so he claimed damages from the council for the costs of maintaining his performers idle while these disputes rumbled on. But this was not the end for the mountebanks. In the next century they were still performing in the Old Town despite the carping of the city's medical establishment. For they still had unwavering support from the public, especially those performers who were the big risk-takers.

For example, there were two performers who saw the Grassmarket as the ideal venue for their brand of entertainment, which was certain to draw large crowds, occupying the large open space available to accommodate them. They were two Italians, likely father and son. Edinburgh had seen mountebanks tightrope-walking before, especially in the High Street at its narrowest points. But in 1733 these two Italians stretched a rope between the Castle's Half Moon Battery and a tall tenement on the south side of the Grassmarket. Surely this was the longest and the highest tightrope ever set up in the Old Town, and below it the largest crowd yet assembled to watch such a performance. Every head was upturned, eyes following the course of the quivering rope.

Then a tremendous cheer went up as the two intrepid acrobats appeared way up on the ramparts of the Half Moon Battery, bowing and waving in acknowledgement. What a reception! And now a great hush as the signal was given for the act to commence. It all happened so quickly. The father, nerves of steel balancing flat out along the taut sloping line, his head forward, shot down it in less than two minutes. The son followed him in the same manner blowing a trumpet all the way. The reaction to this incredible feat from the multitude can be imagined. And just three days later they did it all again, at the request of some prominent citizens who had missed the first performance. Only this time, the father made his way back up the rope to the castle ramparts beating a small drum and firing a pistol on his way. The applause from below was thunderous.

Then he gave a short humorous speech saying that he was now ready to take on the whole Court of Session. But while these Italian daredevils were described as mountebanks, there is no record of them selling medicines, though they most likely did. Or perhaps the combined opposition of the city's physicians and surgeons had at last put an end to that trade. Consider that, at that time, practitioners of the ancient art of herbal medicine, mostly women, could be burned at the stake on Castlehill as witches, especially if their homemade remedies had an adverse effect. All that was needed in such cases was for enough neighbours to testify to some poor woman's involvement with the Devil himself, which they usually did. And the crowds gathered to watch those spectacles as well, at the Witches' Fountain just back there on the esplanade where the burnings took place.

By this time we were back on our main route, coming out of Castlehill into the Lawnmarket. Stuart steered us into Riddle's Court so that he could snap the outside stairs and low-set doorways of this Old Town backland. David Hume had once resided here, while Patrick Geddes inspired its restoration as a place of education and culture by hosting his Edinburgh Summer Meetings. More recently the Workers Education Association was based in the Court.

'Indeed,' pronounced John, not without a degree of solemnity, 'this is a place of education, which reminds me...'

We focussed in like attentive pupils, as John struck a teacherly note.

An Old Town School Story

There is one particular experience which most of us have shared when we were children – the classroom experience, when our formal education began. Well, this is a story of one such experience, an incident which, while it belongs to the history of education in Edinburgh's Old Town, could easily come under the heading of law and order in the Old Town of the 16th century. It is a story that begins with someone who, as an Edinburgh Baillie, had some responsibility for both education and law and order. His name was John MacMorran.

John MacMorran was one of the richest merchants in Edinburgh so he was able to build himself a three-storey mansion of grey stone in the Lawnmarket in 1587. He owned many fine houses in that street but this one was the finest for its time. It was one of the others that stood in a tiny courtyard – Riddle's Court, entered by a close from the Lawnmarket. A fine example of 16th century Scottish architecture – squat, solid, built to last and defendable in times of war.

As well as being a rich merchant, and so naturally a friend of King James vi, who was always broke, John MacMorran was also the Town Council Treasurer, and a magistrate or Baillie as court judges were called. It was in that capacity that on the morning of 15 September 1595 a group of anxious-looking men in black gowns crowded his tiny courtyard seeking his counsel. They were the teachers of the High School – Edinburgh's first grammar school, 100 years old by this time – and their spokesman was the rector himself, Hector Rollock. Baillie MacMorran's first job was to calm the rector down.

Now at this time, not all boys and certainly no girls in Scotland had the privilege of schooling like those of the High School whose parents were of the ruling class – merchants, property owners and the professional classes in general, as well the nobility. But the trouble was that the High School pupils were not too happy with their privileged schooling and were determined to make this clear by rebelling against their sworn enemies – the teachers. So the good Baillie had an idea of what had happened when the troubled deputation of teachers appeared on his doorstep. Yes, he assured them, he would go down to the school again as he had done several times before to lecture the pupils on the necessity of good behaviour – essential for the successful transmission of knowledge.

Yet for all the warnings and threats he would have to deliver down at the High School, in his heart the Baillie felt that the young rebels had a point, and in any case boys would always be boys. He'd been a boy once too. Moreover, he'd listened to their complaints before. They claimed that their school day, from six in the morning until six at night, Monday to Saturday, was far too long, whereas their time off, which was limited to Saints' days and a week in May and September, was too short.

But then again the Baillie also saw that the teachers had a grievance – the sheer frustration of being confined all day to a classroom full of young upper-class pupils of varying temperaments and intellectual abilities. Some of the higher born among them resented being beaten by teachers, who were their social inferiors, and even by other pupils. Then there were those who refused any kind of punishment, offering to fight the teachers instead. Their aristocratic parents could be even more terrifying when shown the poor exam results of their sons and heirs. Obviously, they said, the teachers were not doing the job they were paid to do, which was not much to begin with. Now this was all too much for the beleaguered High School teachers. Some had been driven to despair or to the drink. And now here they were telling Baillie MacMorran that they had been locked out of their school by their rebellious pupils.

All these considerations were buzzing through the Baillie's head as he marched with an air of solemnity and determination down the High Street collecting two of the Town Guard on the way, the High School teachers marching behind them. By the time they reached Blackfriars Wynd which lead to the High School, the Baillie became aware that he was leading a procession, for townsfolk observing the stately deputation had joined it. They had guessed that the popular Baillie had a job to do and had no sympathy with the High School boys whatsoever – they were fed up with their wild bickering, up and down the streets, knocking everything and everybody over, and fighting with rival school boys whenever they were released from school.

Even before the High School came into sight, the noise from it was deafening, and when it did come into sight as they reached the Cowgate, every window in the school was open and full of angry young faces roaring abuse at the world at large until they saw the Baillie and his 'army' marching behind him. At that moment, within seconds, every window was shuttered except one and one boy only at that window. This was redheaded Willy Sinclair, the son of Sir William Sinclair the Chancellor of Caithness. Wild and aggressive, he was a noble not to be trifled with.

Now young Willie was his father's son alright and there he was at the window, his face pale and grim set, looking down at the Baillie, who had ordered the crowd to stay outside the school gates for he had a duty to perform assisted by two Town Guardsmen. So the three of them stood below the open window above the huge barricaded door. Indeed, every door in that school had been barricaded just as the teachers had told him – they had been locked out. The boys had taken over the school and had organised provisions for a siege. They would only surrender, they said, when their demands for longer holidays were met. The teachers had also told the Baillie that the boys were armed. It had all been well-planned.

Even so, the Baillie had his duty to perform, which was not to parley with schoolboys. He had also his reputation to consider and everyone was watching: the crowd and the schoolboys looking through chinks in the shuttered windows. Standing a few feet from the locked door, he looked up at Willie Sinclair at the open window. He knew who he was alright. Who in the Old Town didn't? In those days the Scots spoke Scots. So in his most authoritative voice he called up to the young rebel loud and clear, 'Now Willie Sinclair, there will be nae mair talking or listening till ye open that door!' He was answered immediately by young Sinclair who was now brandishing a pistol which brought screams of alarm from the women in the crowd that had gathered, and a grimness to the face of the Baillie which became even grimmer when the boy called down to him without a waver in his voice: 'Ca off yer men or ah'll pit a ba through yer heid'.

A great hush that could almost be heard came down on the scene. The Baillie never spoke nor moved from where he stood but nodded to the Town Guardsmen who, joined by men from the crowd, brought a huge beam of timber from the builder's yard next to the school. Boom! Boom! Boom! The battering ram pounded the thick solid school door. The door shuddered. The Baillie raised his head and looked up again at the young rebel for some sign of surrender. But the last thing he saw was the pale face of young Sinclair vanishing behind a blinding flash from the pistol pointed at him. One resounding crack and the Baillie lay spread-eagle on the paving stones of the school courtyard, a bright red star on his temple growing bigger by the second. John MacMorran was dead.

More shots rang out but not from school windows. They were shots fired into the air by a full complement of the Town Guard which had just arrived, led by its captain as the furious crowd began to surge towards the school from which boys were now escaping through ground floor windows. Others, huddled in frightened groups, surrendered, and those who had escaped were soon caught and thrown in jail. The body of John MacMorran was carried back to his home in the Lawnmarket through the very door that he had passed through an hour or so before and there he was prepared for burial.

As for the aftermath, the Old Town of Edinburgh was an angry city demanding justice. The MacMorran family especially insisted upon blood for blood and they were too rich to be bought off. But the father of the young killer, Lord Sinclair, made his expected intercession to the King who valued the services and loyalty of his Chancellor of Caithness. Kings were kings in those days, their justice supreme. So in the end it was the King's justice that prevailed, through his royal High Court judges, of course. The Chancellor was ordered to pay a sum of money to the city. The hard core of young revolutionaries – they were only seven in number – were subjected to a severe tongue lashing which it was hoped would mark them for life. It was even rumoured that young Willie Sinclair had his wrists well slapped to teach him a lesson. All in all, not so severe considering that, in those days, men, women and young boys could be hanged for much less.

The fact was, however, that in the eyes of the parents of the High School boys and the education authorities, the real culprits were not the boys but the teachers themselves. They were responsible for the running of the school and the boys' behaviour as well as their education and social refinement, especially the headmaster, Hector Rollock, who was lucky to be just fired. Indeed, the education authorities were for firing all the teachers – only the difficulty of replacing them saved them. So the teachers were kept on but at a reduced salary and were warned that such a tragic happening must never recur. And neither it did, for never again was there a killing.

Nevertheless, just in case the teachers should again prove themselves worthless, a new school rule was ordered: from then on 'no gun powder, fireworks, or firearms of any kind were permitted within the school grounds'. To this day, word for word, that rule remains in the regulations of the Royal High School, as it came to be called.

'Now that's disappointing, John', I complained. 'I wasn't expecting a crime story here.'

'Och,' scoffed Stuart, 'just a bit of high spirits from the young aristos. The real crime is a couple of closes down.'

'Deacon Brodie,' intoned John, 'respectable citizen by day and burglar by night. Not to mention the gambling, cock fighting, pimping and protection rackets. The Deacon had everyone's card marked.'

'He must have known Robert Burns,' I added, pointing to the poet's lodgings on the other side of the street.

'Burns kent the low life and the high,' says Stuart, 'No doubt Deacon Brodie knew exactly who the poet was, and what he was up to.'

'Brodie was a crook right enough. But he's not the biggest Old Town crime story, or the biggest hypocrisy. Remember, this is the city of "Jekyll and Hyde". And Dr Jekyll was a medical man.'

We were both looking at John with renewed interest. But the eyes behind the big spectacles were already fixed elsewhere.

Crime and Medicine

Crime and medicine are two strange bedfellows indeed, for while crime is about harming people, medicine is about healing them. Nevertheless there was a time when they both worked together hand-in-hand, with each mutually benefiting in the process. This was especially true in the 18th century, and even more so in the following one when Edinburgh was considered to be well on its way to becoming the 'medical capital' of the world.

However such progress may not have been so easy to predict in the early 18th century. By this time, while the city had its Royal Infirmary and its Royal Colleges of Physicians and Surgeons, a medical textbook was recommending treatments and prescriptions for various maladies which included a mixture of spiders' webs and the juices of woodlice; crushed skulls mixed with urine; human blood; and horse excrement. Then there was the opening of arteries to draw cups of blood or the use of leeches for the same purpose.

But in the higher echelons of the medical establishment, greater minds – including ambitious ones – knew what was necessary for further progress in the fields of anatomy and the teaching of it. For realistic research, old ideas and beliefs could no longer be relied on. Dead bodies were required for dissection, and the fresher the better.

Now, the surgeons had already come to an understanding with the city authorities on this question. Consequently for research purposes they were allowed so many bodies a year, mainly those of executed criminals. But there were never enough. Enter the 'body snatchers' or the 'resurrectionists' as they came to be called, and soon bodies began to disappear from their graves. The surgeons paid good money for them on delivery. To them it was all in the name of scientific progress. Of course these were all hush-hush backdoor transactions.

Eventually, measures had to be taken to try and stop this gruesome practice, especially with graveyards just outside the Old Town the usual targets. For example, the walls of St Cuthbert's Churchyard were raised to eight feet and its Kirk session appointed an officer to keep records of the dead in a special lodge there. But official gravediggers were still being bribed to leave churchyard gates unlocked, or else these were prised open with specially designed crowbars.

Local reaction to the news that bodies were missing from their graves could be quite fierce, as in the case of that same churchyard in the year 1742 when bodies were reported missing. Citizens gathered to the beat of a drum and marched on the houses of those they suspected, including the Kirk beadle's, and set fire to them. Later, the building of watchtowers and the appointing of night watchmen were to make things less easy for the body snatchers. St Cuthbert's watchtower and the one in the New Calton Burial Ground still stand there today, but of course they are no longer guard posts. Then there were the mortsafes – iron grilles clamped to coffins and buried with them, and other security structures if they could be afforded.

But these protective innovations were not yet in place when two gypsy brothers, Ned and Bob Gurney – called 'Black Bob' because of his swarthy skin and black hair and beard – came up from the Borders to the city to look for work and found there was little or none. The majority of the Old Town population was poor for virtually the same reason. However, it was in the numerous drinking dens in the slum areas of the town that they heard the whisperings that good money was to be had by selling bodies to the city's surgeons – undercover of course. All they needed were two spades and a lantern which they soon acquired.

Now Greyfriars Kirkyard was quite near to the hovel in which they were staying, and they had heard that a burial was to take place there that week. So it was there that they went early on the day before the funeral. The gates were open so Ned and Bob were able to slip into the churchyard unseen with their equipment which included a length of strong rope – the means of their escape over the churchyard wall with the corpse – and they hid these under a clump of laurel bushes. The next day they stood behind all the mourners when the internment took place, and when the mourners had gone they wandered through the churchyard until they found a place to hide until the gates were locked and darkness fell. But, they had also to wait until all the lights from the windows of the tenements overlooking the churchyard had gone out and so total darkness.

The robbers wasted no time. By lantern light they recovered their spades from the bushes and began to dig – an easy enough job for young strong lads especially since the earth was still soft and loose. Soon they were looking down at the coffin lid which they had no trouble prising open, and now they were looking down upon the face of an old lady resting there in peace. Her arms had been placed across her breast, her hands clasped together. But more important for them was the glint of gold on one of her fingers – it was her wedding ring. They could not believe their luck. It might be worth more than the body itself. Quickly, Black Bob stretched down to slip it from her finger but it wouldn't move beyond the knuckle. His brother Ned now took the initiative. He whipped out his jack-knife and began furiously to saw the finger off. Well, what happened now happened within 60 seconds flat.

The corpse sat up with a jolt and a deep groan. Ned leapt high into the air with a scream that could be heard a mile away, and when he came down to earth he made for the churchyard wall just a few yards ahead and cleared it with one leap. But unfortunately for Ned, the outside of the wall was a great deal higher than it was inside – and he made the long descent into Candlemaker Row. When, wakened by Ned's scream, the neighbours in that street reached him, he was dead. He had smashed his head on the cobbles. When they reached the disturbed grave the lantern was still glowing there, and the corpse was still in a sitting position, Black Bob crouching beside it, never moving – his eyes wide open and staring but seeing nothing. He was speechless. At first they didn't recognise him as Black Bob for his hair and beard had turned snow-white. And that was the way they were when he was hanged a week later.

The most efficient body snatching, though, seems to have been done by the surgeons' apprentices themselves. They developed it into a fine art. To begin with, it had to be carried out during the winter months for dead bodies would have been subject to putrefaction in warmer weather. This was why dissection and the teaching of anatomy took place in winter. Also the body snatching itself, as is often imagined, was never done at the midnight hour with owls hooting in the background. The best time was just before 8.00pm when the city police began their night rounds and the graveyard night-watchmen were at their posts. It was then that the gruesome activity began.

A procedure was strictly adhered to. At the coffin head a hole was dug down, the earth carefully emptied onto a canvas sheet. The digging was done with flat spade-like instruments made of wood so that there would be no clinking – iron against stones. Hooks were then lowered to grip the coffin lid at that end and then snapped off; sacking was stuffed down to muffle the sound of breaking wood. The body was then pulled up through the hole, the earth put back, and everything smoothed over to avoid immediate detection. It could all be done within an hour.

Surgeons and their apprentices, however, began to be suspected to such an extent that schools of anatomy as well as houses of particular surgeons were attacked. The Royal College of Surgeons reacted by adding an order to the rules for indentured apprentices, forbidding them to take any part in the stealing of bodies from their graves. But the demand for these, partly due to the rivalry of the top surgeons, continued. Then along came Burke and Hare.

William Burke and William Hare, Scotland's two mass-murderers of the 19th century were in fact Irishmen and had, like many of their countrymen, come over from Ireland to look for work. They worked as navvies on the construction of the Union Canal; but their working partnership really began when they came to live in Edinburgh, in a boarding house in Tanner's Close in the West Port, one of the Old Town's many slums in the early 19th century. It was when Hare, a boarder, married his landlady that Burke with his girlfriend Helen McDougal came to stay there also. But they were not to live there happily ever after.

It all began when Donald, an old army pensioner, died still owing his last week's rent. There was anger all round. Options were discussed. But it was well enough known that good money was to be had selling dead bodies to the surgeons, and the best surgeon to deal with as well. So a coffin was hastily put together by the carpenter in the neighbourhood, wood shavings and other rubbish stuffed into it ready for a mock pauper's burial. Then old Donald's body was wheeled up in a hand-cart to the back door of a school of anatomy in Surgeons' Square where money changed hands and Burke and Hare were now £8 the richer. The buyer of the bodies was Dr Robert Knox, an independent, a sort of maverick member of the College of Surgeons, not quite fully accepted by the medical establishment.

For Burke and Hare it had all been so easy, much easier than body snatching. It got them thinking. Old Donald had not been of much use to anybody, except of course sometimes paying the rent. He did not seem to have had any relatives or real friends. At that time there were plenty of friendless people around, paupers who would never be missed. The problem for Burke and Hare was that they were still alive. But that could soon be remedied.

Burke and Hare were able to pick most of their victims off the streets or scrounging round the lower drinking dens; there was no shortage of these to be found in the West Port, the Grassmarket and the Cowgate. The two 'friendly' Irishmen would select a victim, ply them with drink then it was back to Tanner's Close for more drink until helpless. Then they were thrown onto a bed, their legs held while they were suffocated with a pillow. Late the next night, a body would be delivered to Surgeon's Square – a body bearing no marks of violence. No questions were asked.

It could never have been easier for Burke and Hare the night that a young policeman on duty in the West Port – there was a small jailhouse at the foot of the hill – came across a drunken old woman and was about to lock her up for her own safety. Just at that moment he saw a lone figure making his way up the quiet street. He recognised him as William Burke the cheery Irishman who lodged in Tanner's Close. Stopping him, the young policeman asked Burke if he could find a bed for the old woman in his lodgings else she would have to spend the night in a cold cell – after all, she was Irish just like he was. Burke said he knew her as Mrs Docherty, that he was only too happy to oblige, and taking her arm he went off with her. She was singing like a linty. That was the last time she was seen alive.

If it was the end of Mrs Docherty, it was also to be the end of the gruesome partnership of Burke and Hare – and the end of Burke proper, for when they were murdering her in a backroom of the boarding house she put up a desperate fight. Her shouts and screams through the night woke the neighbours who reported this to the police the next day. They came, and on searching the lodgings they found the body of Mrs Docherty under a bed trussed up like a turkey ready for delivery. Burke and Hare were arrested and charged with her murder. They were also to be charged with 16 other murders, but unfortunately these could not be proved.

The trial began on 24 December 1828, a trial well publicised all over Britain and beyond. Prosecution and defence lawyers were the best legal brains in the land. The defence was led by the brilliant Lord Cockburn. Sir Walter Scott, a lawyer himself, was said to be disappointed that the alleged buyer of the bodies, Dr Robert Knox, was not required to take the stand since, as he claimed, he had never seen the murderers which was quite true. But his trusted night porters had, for it was they who carried out the back door transactions on his behalf.

It was a trial beset with difficulties since the prosecution attempted to convict both Burke and Hare for the other murders they were believed to have committed as well as that of Mrs Docherty, whose body was the only one ever found. Hare and his wife were offered legal immunity if they turned King's evidence. If they testified against Burke, they could go free. They told the truth – 'their truth' of course. So it was Burke alone who on 28 January 1829, faced the hangman in the Lawnmarket before a crowd of 25,000 baying for his blood. After his execution, even more people, 30,000, filed past his body lying there half-naked, like a specimen on a slab in the Old College, for a last look at the despised murderer.

One wonders – was it out of loyalty to Doctor Knox, a popular and brilliant lecturer, that students who watched his dissection of 'Daft Jimmy' and recognised the well-known and likeable simpleton seen alive two days before, said nothing? Similarly there were students who recognised the young and pretty prostitute Mary Paterson lying there dead on the slab awaiting her dissection. Some had enjoyed her company the night before including Knox's cleverest student – who was to become Sir William Ferguson, Scottish Surgeon to Queen Victoria – but nothing was said except among themselves. Such was her beauty that Dr Knox had her dead body sketched by a prominent artist before he went to work on her.

But the law was not quite finished with William Burke. Part of his sentence was that he was to be put on display for all eternity! And the job of stripping his corpse down to his skeleton was given to Knox's arch rival, Professor Alexander Monro and his assistants. In the process, they managed, unofficially I presume, to cut away pieces of Burke's skin which they then had tanned, tinted, polished, and made into snuff-box covers, purses and wallets to give to relatives and friends as 'souvenirs'.

As for William Hare, he was well advised to flee the country immediately after the trial for fear of his life. Some say he lived out his days in the Highlands under an assumed name. Doctor Knox was also obliged to leave the city, especially after an Edinburgh mob attacked his house in Newington and tried to burn it down – the scorch marks on some of the stonework can still be seen today. He too got to London where he tried to resume practice but was virtually ostracised by his profession. He died there an old man in genteel poverty.

But they were all to live on in the many and varying accounts that were written of them, including, of course, 'The Ballad of Burke and Hare', sung on the streets by the balladeers of that time. In the 1930s, children of the West Port and Grassmarket, areas which were described by one writer as the 'Happy Hunting Grounds of Burke and Hare', used to sit together on dark nights on the steps of their winding turnpike stairs and under gaslight swap stories – stories handed down through their families, from grandparents to parents and relatives. There was no shortage of stories from the days when the Grassmarket was once a popular place for public executions, but the story of Burke and Hare was always the favourite.

> Doon the close an' up the stair
> But an' ben wi' Burke an Hare
> Burke's the butcher, Hare's the thief
> Knox the boy who buys the beef.

A sinister echo seemed to sound up Brodie's Close.

'Could we hear something more cheerful now, John?'

The eyes fixed on me with a lugubrious roll.

'We shall proceed down Victoria Street?'

'And?'

'They marched Captain Porteous down here to lynch him, after he ordered the Town Guard to fire on the rioters. That's the real history behind Scott's Heart of Midlothian, as a scholar such as yourself will know.'

'Riots,' agreed Stuart, 'that was the favourite pastime, and just as well given the tyranny folk endured.'

'Yes, riots, but even better, hangings, or at one time burnings'.

John was getting into his stride again, no happy endings guaranteed.

Witchcraft

In centuries past, there was once a time when the worst crime that could be committed was not murder, and those who committed this crime were punished in a very special way and in a very special place. This was just at the foot of the Castle Esplanade where, as we saw today, a bronze plaque marks the spot by the Witches' Well. It would be early in the morning on a chosen day of the week, when huge crowds would be gathered there to hear the crackle of burning timber as flames leapt into the air, and to smell the smell of burning tar and the stench of the burning flesh of those who had committed the worst possible crime, the crime of witchcraft.

They called them witches, accused of talking and listening to the devil, dancing with him and in his name doing people harm, casting spells and curses on them. Such a person, usually a woman, would be arrested and thrown into jail. A trial would follow, usually with plenty of witnesses to testify against her, though more often than not, after being tortured in jail, she would confess to the crime. Then it was up to the Castlehill where she would be tied to a tall stake, timber and tar all around it, and set alight, and everyone watched her burn to a cinder.

But someone accused of witchcraft denying the charge and with few witnesses to testify against her, might be subjected to 'trial by ordeal'. In such a case she would be taken down to the east end of the Nor'

Loch, the long stretch of water which was later replaced with Princes Street Gardens. Then she was tied to a chair at the end of a long wooden plank which was lowered into the loch until the poor wretch was completely submerged. A half an hour or so later, she was pulled up, pulled in and examined. If she was still alive then obviously she was a witch, so it was up to the Castlehill with her to be burned. If she was dead it was equally obvious that she was not a witch. A pity! Still, she was allowed a Christian burial and that was that.

Of course in those days nearly everyone believed in witches. In Scotland, James VI wrote a book about them and burned nearly a hundred of them down in North Berwick. This came about when in 1590 he was sailing home from Denmark with his new queen and his ship was nearly sunk in a storm as it approached the Scottish coast. Witch hunters rounded up a band of so-called witches who confessed – after torture – to having gathered down on the sands of North Berwick and invoked the powers of Satan to whip up a storm that would sink the royal ship. There were men among them as well as two noble ladies – Lady Barbara Napier and Lady Euphemia McLeod – both of whom were pardoned at the very last minute. The rest were hanged, strangled, or burned.

It has to be said that, while most countries in the known world then burned witches, Scotland especially seemed to have really had it in for these women. For example, it is recorded that throughout a period of about 250 years, while England burned 1,000 witches, Scotland, a much smaller country with a much smaller population burned 4,000. It is believed that the last witch to be burned here was Janet Horne in 1722 in the town of Sutherland in the Highlands. At her trial there, witnesses testified that she changed her daughter into a pony and rode it to a witches' gathering where the devil shoed it and danced with Janet. So they burned her. For some time after, some of her neighbours claimed they saw the dead witch on fire, screaming curses at them.

Such claims call to mind the strange case of Major Thomas Weir and his sister, Grizel, who in the later 17th century came to live in a house of two storeys with an attic in the West Bow, now here in the Old Town of Edinburgh. This was before it was extended to join up with the newly built George IV Bridge as Victoria Street. Until then, the West Bow, climbing up from the Grassmarket, ended with a short turn to the left leading to the Lawnmarket. It was once the site of the city's West Gate or Bow. Today, three short flights of steps mark the spot. Among the houses on the opposite side of the street was the house that the Weirs came to live in.

And the Weirs could not have been made more welcome by the community living in that part of the West Bow. It was a strict Presbyterian one – they were called the 'Bow Head Saints' – and the Major had been an officer in the Covenanting Army, then a Captain of the City Guard. When it came to the practice of the Presbyterian religion there was none stricter than the Major. Now a man in his 70s he had become even more rigid. He was soon leading the community at their prayer meetings where his sound grasp of scripture won him great respect. Indeed, they were calling him 'Angelic Thomas', though he didn't quite look like an angel. A tall spare figure, hooked nose and stern features, always dressed in black and never without his staff, there was never any law-breaking with the Major around.

So you can imagine how shocked people were one morning when they heard that the Major and his sister Grizel had been arrested and charged with practising witchcraft. Not quite so shocked, however, were the 'Bow Head Saints'. Not on that morning at any rate, for they had already suffered shock some months before. This happened when they were assembled in the Major's house in the West Bow, where instead of leading them in prayer in his usual ecstatic and inspiring way, he poured out a confession of his past life – one of evil doings which he could no longer hide and for which he must be punished.

His fellow worshippers were shocked alright, and could only conclude that an illness had taken hold of him probably because he had been working too hard and that after a good rest he would soon recover. In the meantime the community, like many religious groups then and since, would keep it to themselves, and thus preserve their good reputation. And so they did, until the Lord Provost, Sir Andrew Ramsay, came to hear of the Major's breakdown and sent doctors to examine him. The medical men found him physically fit but troubled in conscience.

Reluctant to accept the doctors' diagnosis, the Lord Provost then sent two church ministers to see the Major, hear his story, and then report back to him. They did this, but they too suggested that the Major's problem was his conscience, one tortured by the fear of God and no hope of repentance. In sum, it all pointed to a trial as the only way to assess his guilt. So both the Major and his sister Grizel were arrested; from the very beginning his sister had been insistent that she had taken part in all of the Major's evil doings. She also claimed that her mother had been a witch and that she herself had the devil's mark on her brow, while her brother also had the devil's mark, though it was on his shoulder.

So the trial took place but with no-one there to defend the strange pair. The jury found them guilty, though the Major's crime seems to have been more of a carnal nature, one of incest with his own sister rather than witchcraft. Yet it was he who was burned at the stake down at Greenside, Leith Street, before a huge crowd. Refusing to be strangled first, it was reported that he called out, 'I have lived like a beast so let me die like a beast!' Witnesses claimed that his staff, tied to his body, flew up from the flames and vanished into thin air.

Yet Grizel, a self-confessed witch, was not burned; she was hanged in the Grassmarket. Her execution was carried out in great haste, for she tried to strip herself to increase her shame before the great crowd that filled the Grassmarket. So that was the end of Grizel but not, it seems, quite the end of the Major, undoubtedly dead though he was. Neighbours claimed that they saw him late at night striding down the West Bow, his staff bouncing ahead of him. Others saw him galloping down on a black headless horse. They also reported apparitions, shapes and figures flying in and out of the windows of his empty house when darkness came.

The house remained empty for 150 years until a couple moved into it, William Patullo and his wife. But they moved out of it after one night. What drove them out of it was the continual noise, shrieks and loud sighs as well as frightening apparitions throughout the house. No-one else offered to live in it, and this was during a period in the Old Town when poor folk were desperate for shelter never mind a house to live in. So it remained empty until 1878 when it was demolished. Even then there were stories of weird happenings continuing around the site of the old house.

So much for the witches, and those who claimed they saw the terrifying after-death appearances of some of them. Yet those accused of witchcraft and executed did not wear black pointed hats and fly around on broomsticks. More often they looked just like those testifying against them, who were usually their neighbours. Quite often they were the very people the women had tried to help. A so-called witch was usually just someone who used the old herbal cures for sick neighbours or their sick animals, but if the sick neighbour or animal got worse, then whoever supplied the cure was to blame, having been in league with the devil himself to do his work. It was not always understood in those days that while the juices of certain plants and flowers could kill the pain of an illness, overdoses could cause greater pain and even kill the sufferer.

Among the persecutors of witches might be the high and mighty, James VI for example, seeing them as a threat to their power. In general, however, these were times when most people had to endure hardship and misfortune. They felt the need to blame and punish those responsible for this. But who? And for what? The powerless could hardly punish the powerful, or change the bad weather that caused poor harvests. It was much easier to pick on the witches. So the witches became scapegoats.

Eventually this came to an end. But throughout the centuries that followed, the persecution of the innocents who had been branded as witches was not to be forgotten. After all these years, in October 2008, a petition on behalf of thousands of people who had been executed for witchcraft was put before the United Kingdom and Scottish governments, asking for an official pardon for these victims. Experts on the history of witchcraft in Scotland spoke out in favour of the idea, describing these executions as 'legalised murder'.

The fact that many of these so-called witches had actually been trying to do good to people was later recognised when a League of Witches was formed – Wicca, which was first legalised in Britain, and then in America where it is now registered as a state religion. Its aim is to help people not harm them.

'A kind of happy ending then, John

'You must be the judge of that. Only the listeners can tell. Mind you, as we're on the subject of executions…'

Sometimes with John, it's better to keep quiet.

Half-Hingit Maggie

Not all stories have happy endings, but this one does, Donald, though at first it seems a bit grim. Yet that's the way it was to begin with, and it begins up there in the High Street, always a busy street with stalls lining it on either side selling everything you could buy. Big markets were located there too, down closes like Fleshmarket Close and Fishmarket Close.

As with other goods though, fish was also sold in the open streets by street-vendors such as the fishwives. The fishwives were from Edinburgh's fishing villages like Newhaven, Fisherrow and Musselburgh. Their men folk went out to sea and caught the fish – herring, haddock, cod or oysters – and their women packed these into large wicker creels, strapped these onto their backs and carried them all the way to the streets of Edinburgh where the fish was sold to passers-by. Margaret Dickson was one of them.

Margaret, or Maggie as she was more often called, was a small enough but sturdy young lassie – fair hair, a red, weather-beaten face and always a smile on it. She was always sold out by early in the day – people liked her for she was always cheery and nice to the old folk and she would often slip a herring or two into their baskets with a wink in her eye and no charge.

But Maggie had begun to worry, and her friends knew why. She had only been married a year and a half when her husband had gone off to Newcastle nine months ago to look for work. When he had found it, he was to send for her and they would start a new life there. But she had never had any word from him since. They had been so happy together. So what had happened to him? Had he done something wrong and ended up in jail? Or had he been injured in a fight for he did have a

The World Famous **Maggie DICKSONS PUB**

Maggie Dickson's Story

In 1723 Margaret Dickson, a fish hawker in Edinburgh, left town to visit relatives after being deserted by her husband.

On the way south she stopped off in Kelso at an Inn to break the Journey. She stayed a while and worked in return for her board and lodgings. While she was there, Maggie formed a relationship with the landlady's son and fell pregnant with his child.

This was not in her contract of employment, so she concealed the fact that she was expecting and in time the child was born prematurely. When the baby died a few days later, she was determined to throw the body into the River Tweed. Losing her nerve, she laid the baby at the water's edge.

The body was discovered later that day and traced back to Maggie. Arrested and tried under the 1690 Concealment of Pregnancy Act, she was sentenced to be hanged in the Grassmarket Edinburgh on 2nd September 1724.

Maggie was hanged and after her death was pronounced, the body was taken to Musselburgh for burial. On the way there, the funeral heard noises from Maggie's coffin. On opening the coffin they found Maggie to be very much alive.

Recovering to full health, she was allowed to live as it was seen to be God's will that she survive. Living the rest of her days in Edinburgh she was known by all as the celebrated 'Half-Hangit Maggie'!

quick temper? Or was he ill from some disease? Not uncommon in those days.

Now Maggie loved him, so she made up her mind, against the wishes of her parents and friends, to take a bundle of spare clothes, some food, a little money, and go down to Newcastle and look for him. Off she went then, walking mostly with the odd lift or two in a passing trader's cart. On rough roads in those days, it took her nearly two days to reach the border town of Kelso where she stopped at a small inn just outside the town and stayed there for the night. Now it was summer, the inn was busy and the innkeeper and his wife liked the look of Maggie, so they asked her if she would like to stay on a bit as a serving maid. Maggie thought hard. It was a chance here to earn some money which would make things a bit easier when she would be travelling further to Newcastle. It could also help her there too – pay for a room while she searched for her husband.

So Maggie stayed on – a month, two months, three months, nearly four months. Now, she had been happy there. She got on with everybody, but nevertheless felt that it was time to go; she must go and find her husband. But Maggie was faced with a problem that would just not go away. During her stay at the inn she had become friendly with the innkeeper's son – too friendly, in fact. Maggie had become pregnant, and a baby was due in four or five months' time. She told the son; he didn't want to know. She told his parents; they told her to go back home to Musselburgh right there and then. That was the night she cried herself to sleep though she woke again with a terrible pain, a pain as unbearable as the pain in her heart. But Maggie was a strong wee lass – strong enough to put an end to her life, and that was why she left her bed, struggled out the backdoor of the inn into the darkness, and staggered in her nightdress to the River Tweed that flowed nearby.

Poor Maggie just reached the river bank when she fell – the baby was born but born dead! The poor lass was in a daze yet determined to live, so she hid her dead baby deep down among the rushes by the river and managed to get back to the inn. Then, at first light, she packed her bundle and left the inn. But she didn't get far before the Kelso Town Guard caught up with her; a man fishing early that morning on the Tweed had found her dead baby, checked with the innkeeper, and that was that! Back she was taken to Edinburgh and locked up in its dreadful, filthy Tolbooth prison to await trial.

Maggie was then tried, found guilty of the crime of concealed pregnancy and the murder of her child, and sentenced to hang there in the Grassmarket, a popular place of public execution, one week later. On that day in the year, 1724, there was hardly a dry eye in the restless crowd that gathered there to watch her die, to say goodbye. So the hangman did his job quickly and Maggie was pronounced dead.

Now in those days the bodies of criminals were given to the medical authorities to be cut open and examined by surgeons lecturing to young students when learning about the human body, as you know. So the students were in the Grassmarket on that day to collect Maggie's corpse. But so were Maggie's friends from Musselburgh there to collect her body and take it back to her own village for a decent burial. Musselburgh was a town in its own right in those days. So a fierce fight took place; the crowd joined in and the students were driven off. Maggie's friends then put her body in their home-made coffin, tied it down, placed it in a hand-cart, and began the sad journey home pushing the cart all the way back to Musselburgh.

But they soon became tired, having been knocked about a bit during their battle for the body, and so they stopped at Peffermill just outside Edinburgh; leaving their cart outside a small inn there they went in for a quick drink to pull themselves together. Out they came one hour later. But as they walked towards the cart they saw that it was shaking violently, the coffin zigzagging, nearly falling out of the cart. They were terrified, but the bravest one steadied the coffin whose lid had loosened with the movement of the rough journey, and with his jack-knife opened it. There was Maggie alive, her face purple, her fingers red with blood with scraping at the coffin lid trying to get out of the coffin.

Well, they carried her back to the inn, poured a glass of rum down her throat and then another one. The innkeeper's wife washed Maggie clean. Maggie was alive! She had beaten the rope! So it was back in triumph to Musselburgh where she was cheered to the high heavens. But the news travelled fast back to Edinburgh and two days later, once again, she found herself locked up in the Tolbooth jail. But the authorities, angry that the hangman had made a bad job of her hanging, decided to hang Maggie again. But by law she would have to be tried again.

So Maggie found herself once more back in the dock in a crowded courtroom. As she stood there, head down, knowing what would happen, a figure entered that courtroom just before the trial was about to begin and, raising his hand, he called out: 'Stop!' All eyes were upon this small slim figure in an advocate's black robe and silver wig. They knew who he was alright. He was one of the most respected advocates in the city, and soon to become a Lord of the Sessions. So they stopped and listened. His voice rang out loud and clear: 'This trial cannot go on! Does no-one here know that under Scottish law a person cannot be tried twice for the same crime? Especially a person who has already been pronounced dead!' Well, the cheer that went up in that courtroom was deafening, even the hangman, there as a witness, cheered loudly though he had in fact lost his job. Poor Maggie fainted.

Now the end of that story is a well known one. Maggie went home to Musselburgh, especially of course to her village of Inveresk, and a great celebration party. Soon she was back on the streets of Edinburgh selling her fish as cheerfully as ever; and while her neck was a bit twisted due to some small bones broken by the faulty hanging, she was still a fine looking young woman. Since her long-lost husband had been declared legally dead, Maggie married again. She raised a family too, and lived on for another 30 years or so until 1753 when she died an old woman. But during all those years she was no longer known as just Maggie. She was known to everyone as 'Half-Hingit Maggie'!

'Happy now?' grinned Stuart, 'sometimes John keeps you hanging on, to coin a phrase, but he always delivers.'

Coming back up Victoria Street, we crossed George IV Bridge, passed the site of the last public execution in Scotland at the corner, and stood looking at St Giles Cathedral dominating the heart of the Old Town with its wonderful crown steeple, and its bells. And behind it the stern sweep of the Law Courts. We followed John's eyeline upwards.

'Looking through old burgh records and chronicles can often be a boring experience, beset at times with frustration.' And this from the man who had gone back to University as a mature student to come to grips with history. 'Past incidents recorded in such a matter of fact way, and the language archaic. If you're not careful, you can miss a story that would have headlines in today's newspapers.'

'Such as?'

'This one for example.'

The Bell Ringers

It concerns two young men who were destined to share the same fate from the very first time they met as labourers working on the building of Edinburgh's New Town in 1776. Both had much in common – they came from large poor families with widowed mothers, were poorly educated, but were young and strong. They also shared a wonderful dream and we will come to that dream presently.

Hamish Munro had come down when a boy from the far north with his family to Edinburgh's Old Town. About the same time, Malachy O'Shea had come over from Ireland with his family. As labourers they were now employed by a local builder, Simon McMean, who like other local builders was making good money from all the New Town construction going on at that time. But McMean's labourers were always poorly paid and were often laid-off work for periods when New Town construction was held up.

It was the time of 'Edinburgh's Golden Age' when Scotland's cleverest people were gravitating towards the capital – an age of ideas when great advances in the arts and sciences were being made. But Hamish and Malachy saw nothing golden about all this; for them, Edinburgh was a decaying old town reeking with smoking chimneys and even more odious stenches when the cries of 'Gardyloo' signalled the time of night for the emptying of brimming chamber pots from windows onto the streets below.

The really well-off seldom walked Hamish and Malachy's filthy streets – they just hailed the taxis of the day, sedan chairs. They were carried mostly by big strong Highland men wearing their official badges of the Sedan Chairmens' Society. They earned good money but were known to swear at passengers who didn't pay them enough, though they swore in their native Gaelic, which of course was a foreign language to those passengers who just smiled back politely when they were being cursed.

To become sedan chairmen was the dream shared by Hamish Munro and Malachy O'Shea. But how could it come true for them? Where was the money to come from that would buy a sedan chair made by a skilled cabinet maker? They asked their employer for a loan, assuring him that he would be paid back soon, but he laughed them to scorn and the next time there was a delay in New Town building, he sacked them.

It was then that Malachy became inspired – he had an idea! Malachy was always having ideas. He was the smarter of two, or so he believed. Hamish listened to his plan in part amazement and part horror. But they had always stuck together through thick and thin so he fell in with it. It was a plan that was to land both of them in the Tolbooth Jail, and then the Court of Session on a charge punishable by hanging.

The courtroom in Parliament Square was filled to capacity on that morning of November 1788, when the two prisoners were brought in. One arrived flat-out on a stretcher. The other heavily bandaged, limped in on crutches. Lord Newton was presiding – that God-fearing, hard-drinking old judge, renowned for his harsh sentencing – and hanging was his speciality. He sat there expressionless when the charges against the wretched prisoners began to be read out, though he shook his head in disbelief as he listened to some of the details. Surely these two criminals were quite insane he thought as he finished off the bottle of claret that was always near to hand on the bench. Lord Newton swore to his friends that it helped him make the right judgements.

He looked down with contempt on Hamish and Malachy and snapped at them to answer the charges against them, but they were incoherent when they tried to speak between whimpers of pain. Now it was just then that a young advocate, Henry Cockburn, later Lord Cockburn, begged his lordship to let him speak in their defence with the usual eloquence for which he was to become famous. Lord Newton muttered to himself then nodded impatiently, but as he listened, his face took on a look of utter incredulity. Yet the only time he interrupted the young advocate was when he hammered the bench to silence the shouts of derisive laughter that burst throughout the courtroom at what was being heard. After all, even though he had already decided to hang the prisoners, he knew it was only right that they should be given a fair trial first.

So then, the defending advocate, Henry Cockburn, told their story. He made it clear that both young men were not theologians and so could get their morals confused. Both young lads – their mothers widowed – were trying to support their families by working for an employer who paid them poorly and sacked them after they had asked him for a loan of money to buy a sedan chair, for they only wanted to earn an honest living. It was then that in desperation they decided, wrongly of course, to 'steal' a loan from his fifth storey house in the Lawnmarket. They didn't see this as stealing since they had firm intentions of paying McMean back – in secret, of course. But, said Cockburn, there was no point in describing their plans as to how they were going to steal the money, for that never happened. Something else happened instead.

Indispensable to Malachy and Hamish's plan was a strong rope, at least 30 feet long, but this had proved impossible to acquire. Strong rope was costly and the builders who used such ropes would not lend them one. So as well as being unemployed the lads were now disconsolate and despairing, as they sat one morning on the steps of St Giles Cathedral bemoaning their lot. Perhaps, said Malachy, a prayer might help, so they entered the church. Now they had just sat down to pray

when the church bell began to toll out the hour of 12.00 noon. It was then that it came to Malachy, like most of his ideas, in a flash! 'Hamish,' he said, 'the bell, the bell, a rope, a rope!'

'Oh no!' said Hamish.

'Oh yes! said Malachy, 'we have just prayed and the Good Lord is ringing out his answer. He knows we only want to borrow the rope.'

Hamish saw the point, but the church was hardly the place to discuss it so off they went to a quiet close. Their heads were buzzing, especially Hamish's.

They were back with their polished plan in the early evening and they went into the church, which was conveniently empty. When they were sure of this, they slipped into a side altar and hid there until late when the beadle arrived and locked the great church door from the inside, leaving the key in the lock, as was his practice before he went off to bed in his small bedchamber at the back of the church. But to their consternation, he had also locked the door of the narrow spiral staircase that led up to the belfry from which hung the bell, its rope dropping to the floor. Yet, for one reason or another, he did not leave the key in that door.

Now this meant that they could not get up to the belfry as they had planned, where they could have cut the bell rope. It would then have fallen to the floor and been theirs to be off with – not the whole 70 feet of it, 30 feet was all they needed. So what were they to do? This had not been planned for. They just stood there staring at the rope which ended in a coil on the floor right where they stood. Also they might well have been in pitch darkness for they had forgotten their lantern, but a great beam of moonlight shafted down through the window of the bell tower spotlighting the scene.

So were they beaten? No, for it came to Malachy in a flash as his eyes followed the ascending rope until it disappeared into darkness. 'Hamish', he whispered, 'Hold the rope steady so the bell won't ring. I'm going up.' And up he climbed, a sharp knife between his teeth. A young fit lad, he was halfway up in seconds, then he stopped and looked down. Below his feet was all the rope they needed. Two lightening slashes of his sharp blade and the rope below him fell, but it fell on Hamish, crashing him to the stone floor nearly knocking him out.

'Get up!' shouted Malachy, now dangling 30 feet up. 'Come down!' shouted Hamish trying to free himself from below the heavy pile of rope that fallen on him. Then it came to the quick-thinking Malachy in another flash – he would cut the rope above him instead of below him, and that is exactly what he did next. Two lightning slashes above him and he came down alright, but right on top of Hamish who had just staggered to his feet. And now the great bell was ringing amid loud cries of pain as the beadle in nightcap and gown arrived on the scene, a lighted candle in each hand, hurrying to unlock the church door which was now being pounded on by the Town Guard for the bell was still ringing loudly and wildly.

Malachy and Hamish, both unable to move, were carried to the Tollbooth jail next door. And now two days later here they were in the courtroom, one on a stretcher, one on crutches. After telling their story, Henry Cockburn summed up his defence: 'Just look at them,' he said, 'their heads bowed with shame and remorse. Yet after what you have heard can you really call them criminals? In the end what did they really steal? Nothing! Are they capable of stealing anything? Treated badly by their employer, all they wanted to do was to find a means of supporting their widowed mothers and families. My lord, I rest my case.'

The honourable Lord Newton smashed the bench again to silence the cheers that followed Cockburn's speech for the defence. 'I've heard enough,' he roared as he reached for his black cap, but it was only to shift it away from the second bottle of claret that had been placed on the bench for his next case. Ignoring the prisoners, he now addressed the court.

'I am sure,' he said, 'that Henry Cockburn would agree that if both prisoners had one ounce of brains between them they could be a danger to themselves and to the community. However, I have come to the conclusion that instead of hanging them, which they richly deserve, or sending them to the Bedlam, where they truly belong, I place them under order, as soon as they are fit for work, to submit their future earnings to the church to pay for the repair of the bell rope. And, I may add, I have no doubt that, given time, they will manage somehow to hang themselves without any assistance from me or this court.' For once, as cries of 'Amen, Amen!' came from the gallery, Lord Newton spared his hammer and the bench.

Well, in the end, Malachy and Hamish did get well and did get work, and soon paid their debt to the church as ordered. But to their complete bewilderment, after they did this they received an anonymous letter instructing them to call in at a cabinet maker in the Lawnmarket and collect a brand new sedan chair. They had, of course, to sign a paper agreeing to pay it up over a fixed period of time. Now it did not take very long for Malachy O'Shea and Hamish Munro to become the fastest and most reliable sedan chairmen in the Old Town. And though they never discovered who their mysterious benefactor was, they did think it a bit strange that their very first customer was that fearsome judge, Lord Newton, who continued his patronage of their services to the end of his days. While they both agreed never to accept his fare, he never ever offered it.

John's story had taken us from Kirk, court and prison to the street life of Old Edinburgh. Coming round the north side St Giles, where the site of the Heart of Midlothian – the former Tolbooth Jail – is marked in stone, we arrived at the Mercat Cross, once the centre of High Street bustle. Here the merchants traded, beggars begged, hawkers hawked, and street artists busked. Here at the height of the Enlightenment, according to an enthusiastic Frenchman, you could shake 50 men of genius by the hand. But John's eye was on the buskers, past and present, not the philosophers.

Monkey Mary and Co

Hokey Pokey was a hardworking member of Edinburgh's Italian community at the end of the 19th century. Italy's unification had not solved all its problems, political, social or economic. Italians, especially from the rural south, were shipping out, bag and baggage, to try for a better life in the more industrialised countries. And that was how Hokey ended up in the Old Town's High Street – a pioneer in the art of making and selling ice-cream, from his home-made wooden barrow. In old pictures of him, a tiny urchin waits eagerly for Hokey to serve him an ice-cream, but not in a cone! Ice-cream then was sloshed into a hand-twirled piece of thick brown paper – a poke! And that's why Hokey was Pokey, and 'Hokey Pokey' was painted in large white uneven letters across the sides of his barrow.

But Edinburgh's Italian immigrants brought more to its Old Town streets than ice-cream, or fish and chips for that matter. What the Italians brought especially to Old Town Edinburgh from their hillside villages and small towns was their music. But not to its theatres or concert halls – they brought their music to its open streets. Of course in doing this they were adding to an already old and established tradition of Edinburgh's street entertainment, and the Italian contribution was a welcome one, helping to lighten up the drabness and depression that could that characterise much of life.

When the Italians came here, they brought their musical instruments with them. Many of these instruments had been handed down through family generations together with the skills required to play them. Mandolins, guitars, fiddles, harps, trumpets and piccolos – instruments that had been played in their village and small town bands, played at births, weddings, funerals and festivals. So here was the seemingly uncultured poor of the Old Town listening, whether they knew it or not, to snatches of arias and choruses from the music of Italian composers like Verdi, Donizetti, Puccini and so on – and they liked it! They would often whistle it. And later some of them during wartime experience in Italy, were hearing it again.

But the Italian and now Scots-Italian serenaders played on, big families of them like the Fuscos from the Cowgate and Pleasance – there were 13 of them and every one could play a instrument! The D'Angelos, Marinos, Gargaros from the Grassmarket, the Paccitis from the Lawnmarket and Tollcross. Playing also those haunting Neapolitan and Sicilian folksongs. Then the great piano accordion arrived virtually replacing the 'Button Box' though they also called this the 'Box'. And it was a big box indeed – silver ornamented and brightly coloured, flashing ivory keys and different makes, all with Italian names – the Scandali is the one name I remember.

These were bought at Pagano's music shop in Grindlay Street, paid up at five shillings a month or one shilling a week. So in this way a new sound came to the Old Town streets – that great spread and stream of rippling notes between thundering chords. Now classical marches, waltzes and by this time, jigs and reels – Scotch and Irish – were playing a prominent part in the Italian busker's repertoire, as well of course as the film and record hits of the '30s and '40s. The street singer or chanter was becoming indispensable, singing above an accordion, the open street his stage, no microphone – lungs of iron.

The younger Italians were growing up. Jobs were hard to come by in the '30s and here was money to be made in the town and touring beyond it. In consequence, the street stage became quieter – instrumentally that is, but with one exception which went on and on. A lady this time, with an instrument or machine that must have been the oldest – certainly the biggest – that the Italians had brought with them to the Old Town in earlier days. Its sound was incomparable and difficult to describe. It was a sound that could bring children running out of closes and back greens – the girls to dance around the machine that was making it, the boys to goggle at Smokey the monkey with tunic and cap that danced upon it, and all of them to stroke and pat the small pony between the shafts that pulled this piano-shaped box on wheels.

The box that poured out this merry, gurgling, bell-like sound that was like no other was, of course, a barrel organ. In the early years of this century, it was the property of the dark-haired young woman who turned its handle. And she, to the Old Town at large, was known as 'Monkey Mary', but to her Grassmarket neighbours she was also known as Angela Vareechi. She was to go on for a long time, despite the persuasions of her successful hairdressing sons who retired from the streets. Anyway there was not a youngster then who would not have loved to have turned the handle of that machine, or to have solved the mystery of what – or who – inside it was making that magical sound.

Years later it still remained a mystery to me, even when I was told that the handle turns a cylinder or barrel inside the box which is first inset or 'fixed' with a series of pins which engage the piano keys. So it followed then that the real genius behind the scenes was the 'fixer' – the fixer of the pins, and he was real enough for he stayed in the same close as Angela Vareechi, or 'Monkey Mary'. He was a tall moustachioed Italian with a really bad limp – Earnesto Tomasso Molle, a disabled ex-officer in the Italian army. His passport described him as a musician and portrait painter, but he was more than that. Back home, he had been the village scribe; the neighbours depended on him – he could read and write! And now in the Grassmarket they still depended on him, as, of course, did 'Monkey Mary'.

'Monkey Mary' had other back-ups especially when her profession, in the summer months, took her well beyond the city boundaries. On such occasions, as well as the pony and organ went two turtle doves in a cage, two bull terriers and her nephew – a young man whom Mary had brought up. We used to follow the pony's course as it pulled the barrel organ down King's Stables Road when Mary was heading for the New Town with her more classical renderings. We would have fits of laughter when halfway down this long street, Smokey would suddenly stop, head down, refusing to move. Mary would go through her routine – whispering in its ear, pulling its ear, a smack with a stick. No, Smokey was not for moving. Then Mary standing back would swear at it in her best Italian, and as only a Grassmarket Italian could swear, and when she stopped for a breather, Smokey would start up. On they would go.

Now in the world of children with increasing years comes increasing awareness, until, of course, they grow up, which could mean never grow up! I mean, here we were, young children calling Smokey's mistress 'Monkey Mary', but there was no longer a monkey in sight. So it came to pass that I asked the question, 'Whatever happened to Monkey Mary's monkey?' 'The monkey died just before Angela Vareechi died. Don't you remember? Ah, your Monkey Mary is the second Monkey Mary. She is Mary Diplacido who became Mrs Dunlop. Sure enough you would have been too young to remember when she took over from Angela Vareechi – but you were there all the same and anyway you're still listening to the same music from the same barrel organ.'

So it had been a case of the queen is dead, long live the queen! And our queen, our Monkey Mary, lived on long enough, just long enough for my two children to dance to the music of her barrel organ. Then this unique strand of an old tradition of street entertainment ended about 1966 when Monkey Mary 2, Mrs Dunlop, died and Smokey aged 23 went off to spend his last days on a farm in Balerno, where he could dream in peace of cheering audiences at the King's Theatre without being sworn at – in Italian.

Well, 20 or so years went by. I had grown older but was not quite finished asking questions and one still remained to be answered, 'Whatever happened to the barrel organ?' Maybe I had left it too late. Those who would know, the oldest Italians, had been slipping away. Lucky for me old busker, Joe D'Angelo, was still around, though he did not have long to go either. Old Joe's information took me to the Canongate, to a shop selling modern keyboard instruments. Yes, an old barrel organ had been on display there. More information, and this took me to the top of a five-storey, 18th-century tenement in the High Street – The Museum of Childhood.

And there it was, on the top floor in the far corner of a long dimly lit room – subsequently placed nearer the door. I nearly missed it for the casing had been stripped of its mysterious waterproof covering that had once tightly bound it. About four feet high but solid. The first time I had seen the barrel without its skin – and it did look a bit forlorn. We were both alone in that room and for me that barrel organ rolled back centuries. There was no-one there for whom I could sing its praises.

Nevertheless, hanging on the wall beside it was a small framed picture of the barrel organ in action, Monkey Mary 2, Mrs Dunlop, was turning the handle, but there were no children dancing around, for it was the New Town. Only Smokey was there, head down – I could guess where his thoughts were. And below the picture were a few lines referring to them both, though nothing about Mary and the Monkey.

I have the very same picture at home, but hanging beside it is another one, a big one too. Its background is the lower West Bow of the early 1900s, and there turning the handle of the barrel organ is Monkey Mary 1 – a dark-haired Angela Vareechi. The monkey is a blur but clear enough are the children dancing around her on the cobbles.

Before I left that room I looked around, we were still alone, the barrel organ and I. I looked down for the handle but it was gone. Well, no harm then to give its top a gentle rap just before I go, I don`t know quite why, maybe a secret wish that it would suddenly start to play for me. But how could it? Then again, there is this thing called delayed action, for when I left the building and began to climb the High Street – always that noise of cars, buses and people – I heard none of it. All the way home all I could hear was the rollicking, laughing, jangling sound of Monkey Mary's barrel organ.

We stood listening together to that music for a moment.

'This was the bit,' commented Stuart, 'down to the Tron and Hunter Square. Perfect for busking now too since it was blocked off to cars.'

'And the buskers, street artists are back, not just at Fringe time, and from across the world.' I agreed, wondering why everything goes in cycles. John's gravelly voice brought me back to the street.

'Mind you, there was a Fringe then too, when it came to theatre, and the fringe of a fringe.'

Suddenly, I knew where this was going. 'Will you tell us about Ned Holt, John?'

Ned Holt

Every city, town or village has its characters. I mean those individuals who for one reason or another are not quite like the rest of us. I don't mean those who try so hard to be different from everybody else. I mean those who can't help being different. Such people were – and still are – often described as odd balls, cranks, nutcases, sometimes more kindly as eccentric. They are found in all social classes, from royalty to peasants, from princes to paupers.

One Edinburgh artist in the 18th century made his name recording them in pen and pencil though in his time, the self-taught artist never became as famous as he should have. He was John Kay – he lived and worked in the High Street where he was able to spot the Old Town's characters and draw them as he saw them. Today, Kay's portraits are a collection of meticulous drawings prized by all Edinburgh's local historians.

John Kay was succeeded in the 19th century by another self-taught Edinburgh artist who never dreamed that his watercolour sketches of Old Town characters – they were mostly common people of the street which he would often dash off in a tavern to pay for his drink – would ever be sought and bought by collectors long after he had gone. His name was Edward Holt, more familiarly known as Ned. I had heard his name when a boy. Ned Holt and other well remembered street characters were often the subject of humorous reminiscences at family gatherings. But I can't remember anything said of Ned as an artist.

Yet round about 1960, after having watched Saturday's Hibs v Hearts match at Tynecastle, I was standing pint-in-hand, in a crowded Gorgie pub called the 'Worthies', peering through the smoke at a small framed picture in a far corner of the pub. At that time I was trying to paint pictures myself. I got closer to it. For the first time I was looking at a faded water colour painting by Ned Holt – signed by him. Not one of his many single pictures of the Old Town characters, but a group of them, placed by him in line against a background of St Giles in Parliament Square. I am sure it was an original. Much later I was to acquire copies of Ned's work including that one. Anyway the picture!

First in the line, extreme left in the picture, standing to attention in the uniform of a Highland regiment is Toby Gunn, Edinburgh's famous recruiting sergeant with a distinguished war record in India and Egypt. Toby Gunn boasted that he had recruited half the British army by friendly persuasion in his recruiting office which was a pub in the Lawnmarket called the 'Indies'. The back-patting recruiting sergeant would buy his unsuspecting quarry a pint of ale, which was drank with a relish until the poor sap discovered that at the bottom of the glass was the 'King's Shilling', a soldier's first-day pay. There was no escape and he had to enlist. But the wily sergeant did not like to be reminded of the time in that very bar he had recruited a man with a wooden leg.

After the sergeant comes dainty Oyster Nell in her traditional fishwives clothing and creel strapped to her back. Always surrounded by the young dandies she would be sold out within an hour of standing in the street, the young men being as stimulated by her pretty face and ankles as they would be by her oysters. Next, Big Blind Hughie the street vocalist, who, if he was singing at the top of the Royal Mile could be heard clearly at the bottom. Next to him old Register Rachel with her stick – white bonnet, hollow band and long flowing dress. Everyone knows her story. How when as a pretty young woman she had waited outside Register House dressed in her best for her young love to appear; they were to be married that morning, but he never came that morning nor any other morning after. But she did, the next morning and for all the mornings after. In her breast, hope sprung eternal. For the rest of her life she brought her stool and sat there outside Register House, sometimes selling matches.

Beside Rachel in the picture stands the small baker's assistant whose nose resembled the shape of the scones he sold, so they called him 'Scone Nose'. Beside him is the even smaller hunchback they called 'Candle Doubt', which means the stump of a candle. In front of him standing on a chair nearest to St Giles dressed in his long black coat, tall hat and white spats a lit lantern in his hand is 'Daddy Flockhart' the archetypal 'fire and brimstone' street preacher. He was a match for those who would heckle and torment him shouting his nickname 'Burn the Bible'. But ever ready for them he would roar back at them 'if a hud a thousand bibles, I'd fire them from Mons Meg in the Castle doon the length o' the High Street'. But sweeter notes came from the last two figures in that picture. Arm-in-arm, with overcoats and hats, one with a stick, these last two were a popular street singing duo, the blind vocalists David Arkley and Jamie Mann.

Yet it seems that Ned Holt had never aspired to become an acknowledged artist. His only lessons in Art were from a Town Square publican, an amateur artist who saw that Ned had natural talent. For Ned, sketching the locals was only a side line. It was beer money. His real ambition was to become a performer. He began as a showman, and turned his hand to running Penny Shows on Grassmarket fair days, at which he displayed his living skeleton and it danced – along with the petrified Mummy and the headless lady. Then he graduated to performing as an actor in the Old Town's 'Penny-Gaffs' – the poor man's theatre, and actually the forerunners of the music halls. Perhaps Ned hoped he might graduate further and perform some day in the New Edinburgh Theatre at the Synod Hall, or at the Lyceum newly opened in Grindlay Street, where the city's upper class flocked to watch the greats like Henry Irving and Ellen Terry up from London to perform Shakespeare.

But that was not to be. Nevertheless he remained the King of the Penny-Gaffs where he played in melodramas like *Sweeney Todd: The Demon Barber of Fleet Street*, *The Polish Jew* and *Rob Roy*; but also abridged versions of Shakespeare. The crowd in these small and shabby venues adored Ned Holt. No actor could die like Ned. He made dying last a long time. When he would at last die, especially as Hamlet, the audience would shout for him to die again. His success at these venues must have been quite an accomplishment when you consider the audience members could, before they entered the theatre, buy rotten fruit and vegetables from barrows lined up outside for the express purpose of throwing them at performers who incurred their displeasure.

J. Wilson McLaren, Scots poet and writer, recalls Ned Holt returning home after playing Hamlet at that Gaff to his lodgings in White Horse Close, and stopping here at the Tron where he found the blind vocalists David Arkley and Jamie Mann singing to a small crowd. Doffing his

shabby cap with a great sweep and bow, he addressed the crowd in a melodramatic voice, 'Ladies and Gentlemen, the Prince of Denmark does not consider it beneath his dignity to go round with the hat'. And he did, making a good collection for his friends in adversity.

Ned Holt was to die for the last time, not on stage, but by the roadside one night after the Musselburgh Races. I was unable to discover where he was buried.

So, just some Old Town characters or eccentrics if you like, who once walked its streets, though the word 'eccentricity' I have never really been able to understand. I say 'all the world is queer except thee and me and even thee'.

As I knew, Ned Holt is a hero of John's, as an artist and performer rooted in the Old Town. Many of his pictures have been preserved in Edinburgh City Libraries.

'For a country that suppressed theatre for so long time, there was a lot of it about,' Stuart commented.

'Not everyone was devoted to John Knox, not hereabouts anyway,' said John with a quizzical look in my direction, knowing my familiarity with the reformer.

By this time, crossing the Bridges we were passing another Old Town haunt, Carubber's Close, where in 1736 Allan Ramsay opened the first official theatre in Edinburgh since the Reformation, only to have it closed down by the City Council. On the other side of the road is Blackfriars Street, where James vi had a special theatre built for Shakespeare's company to perform on tour. That was before he went to London as James I and became patron of 'The King's Men'. Yet, as John tells it, the unofficial theatre tradition went on uninterrupted. So he is not for stopping at Carubber's Close, but moves on with steady intent to another close on the north side of the High Street, nearly opposite Blackfriars Street, to contemplate a different kind of hero.

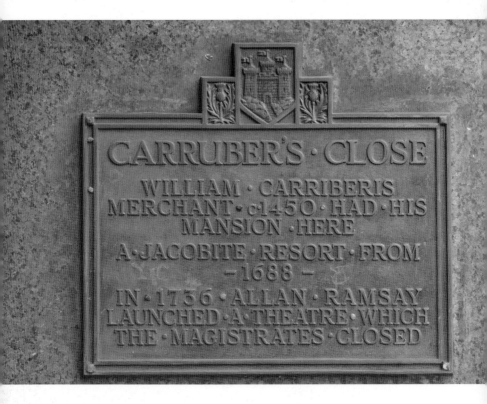

A High Street Hero

This high stone tenement with its traditional crow-stepped gable takes in numbers 97 to 103, and it stands between two closes – Paisley Close and Baillie Fyfe's Close. It was built in 1862 when it replaced a much older one dating from the 17th century; an old tenement of five storeys and attics towering almost a hundred feet into the air, built with timber and later faced with stone. A tenement once occupied by wealthy Edinburgh citizens, it came by the 19th century to be filled with large families of the poorer classes.

People passing up and down the High Street on 23 November 1861, who bothered to give it a glance, were seeing it for the last time, for by 1.30am the following morning, its front section facing the High Street had gone. At that early hour of the morning, neighbours were awakened by the sound of its going – a deep thunderous rumbling followed by one almighty crash. The sound brought two patrolling policemen hurrying to the spot as well as half-dressed neighbours from the trembling tenements that had flanked it, soon joined by a greater number of High Street people.

But there was nothing to see except the dense clouds of black dust that hid the mountain of rubble and debris from which it was rising, and from which pitiful cries for help could be heard. People were trapped amidst the timber and stone of this decaying tenement which had collapsed within itself. There was, however, no sound coming from those who were buried deep at the bottom of the pile.

The police were quick to alert the fire brigade who were on the spot almost immediately. But it was only by removing the tops of the street lights, now blazing gas torches, that they were able to gauge what kind of rescue could be attempted without further endangering the helpless victims who were still alive. In that regard the High Street locals had to be restrained, especially those with relatives amongst the victims, from pulling people whether conscious or unconscious bodily out of the wreckage with their bare hands.

The High Street tragedy of 1861 cost 35 people their lives, while many more were maimed or injured. The collapse vindicated the warnings of social reformers like Dr Henry Littlejohn whose reports, supported by a sympathetic Lord Provost called William Chambers led to the first City Improvement Act in 1867. This led to demolitions, not all of them necessary, and to rebuilding. Yet even in the 1950s and '60s rack-renting landlords left old Edinburgh tenements in a dangerous condition.

But the tragedy here was also added to the treasure trove of Old Town stories kept alive on the street, on stair-heads by the womenfolk, and in the neighbouring taverns – stories such as the policeman in the tenement who was out on night duty and survived, but lost his life savings of 40 gold sovereigns that he had drawn from the bank that day in order to emigrate to Australia. Or the miraculous escape of the Baxter family, all 11 of them, because their father, the only one awake, heard 'a rumble of chuckie stanes' and, after wakening his family, got them out the back seconds before the crash.

But even more miraculous was the very last rescue. It had taken days to clear the rubble in search for bodies, dead or alive, and it was just as they were ending their last day of search that toiling rescuers heard a muffled sound coming from a small pile of remaining wreckage. Coming nearer they heard the faintest of cries. It was a cry for help which became slightly louder when the pile was being carefully cleared. And there he was, crouched in a cellar-like cavity, trapped by a huge beam and wedged in by broken stones. Well, they got him out at last – a small wisp of a boy, covered from head to foot with black and grey stone dust, bruised but unbroken in body and spirit.

He was young Joseph McIvor who, of course, became the local hero, for there in his entrapment beneath the pile, he could well have died of suffocation or lack of water, or of shock and fear itself throughout the long days of the searching. The authorities considered this young lad worthy enough to have his memory kept alive by a sculpted portrait of his head on a stone plaque set above the entrance to Paisley Close, next to the tenement that had replaced the collapsed one. Below the sculpted portrait, inscribed in stone are the words of the young lad's cry for help heard by his rescuers: 'Heave awa lads I'm no deid yet'. Indeed, when as children we played in and out that close, we never called it Paisley Close – we called it the 'Heave Awa Close'.

And that could be the end of this short story, with Joseph McIvor living happily ever after, and maybe it should be. But one cannot help wondering what eventually happened to the High Street laddie, the hero. What seems to have happened is that after losing his parents and family in that High Street tragedy, young Joseph – he was only 13 years old – was befriended by the Lord Provost. He was offered entry to George Heriot's school and home for orphans, after which he would have been sent to learn a trade. But it is believed that he rejected this in favour of signing on as a cabin-boy on a merchant sailing ship bound for faraway places. It was also believed that a year later, he went down with that ship when it was lost in a storm of the coast of Jamaica, drowned with the rest of the crew.

Now if that was the case, then who was Captain Joe? That was the only name the neighbours knew him by – an old retired sea captain who 50 years later had come to live in the attic flat of the tenement that had replaced the old collapsed one. No-one in the neighbourhood really got to know him. He kept himself to himself – virtually a recluse, and a solitary drinker with strong black Jamaica rum delivered regularly to his door. Often late at night his neighbours would hear him singing to himself as he made his way down the stairs on to the street. He went no further and always did the same thing – stopped singing, looked up at the sculpted plaque above the entrance to Paisley Close, and staggered back up the stair.

That was Captain Joe, the only name he was known by. No-one knew
his surname, not until three years after his arrival at the close when one
night they found him lying dead at the close entrance. Police searching
his belongings identified him as Captain Joseph McIvor.

> Stuart was still photographing the sculptured head above Heave Awa
> Close, and muttering about rack-rent landlords, as John headed across
> the street to the Museum of Childhood, with me trailing in his wake.

> Our guide was now in flow, rehearsing some of his favourite tales,
> often requested on walking tours or at the Guid Crack Storytellng
> Club in the Waverley Bar. No need for prompts or questions.

The Doll

The story here is about a doll, a rather unusual doll that came into
existence in an unusual way. We are in the late 19th century in the Old
Town, when the parents and grandparents of my generation were old
enough to have heard this story, and in later years to pass it on.

It was a period which in social terms saw many improvements, but
times were still hard for too many of the poorer classes. It will save
description if I compare those Old Town days with the London of
Charles Dickens at that same period, though on a smaller scale. *Hard
Times*, *The Old Curiosity Shop* and *Oliver Twist* describe the social
conditions prevalent in the London of his time. Dickens himself noted
the similarity to Edinburgh during his well-recorded visits to our capital.

Now it is the case that when a population or a community has to
endure hardship and poverty, it is usually the children who suffer most.
No-one saw this more clearly than the minister who fresh from a
country parish came to serve in an Old Town one. He was appalled at

what he saw – throughout the day, hordes of children running here and there, up and down the streets their rags flying in the wind, shouting, cursing, with faces pale and thin, only stopping to beg. Edinburgh's Old Town saw a great increase in begging despite attempts to discourage it but usually a blind eye was turned in the children's case. The minister saw the children late at night – sleeping in closes and stairs, stone steps for pillows. He spoke to them; they spoke to him.

Well that minister's name was Dr Thomas Guthrie, and he tried to do something about these street children. First he set up what you might call a children's soup kitchen in a Victoria Street basement, like an early day Mary's Meals, and the children came – orphans and virtual orphans. They gobbled up the food and were tempted into learning something of the three Rs – reading, writing and arithmetic – along with a bit of religion. And so Dr Guthrie's first 'Ragged School' began, shifting later to new premises on Castlehill where the buildings can still be seen. Guthrie's schools and homes went on to make their own history.

All that being said, and necessarily so for our story, I can now go on to introduce Rosie Gale. Rosie was only five years old when her young mother died of tuberculosis in their single room in a hovel in the Cowgate during one of the city's regular epidemics of that disease. Rosie had never known a father, she had no relatives, and so now she was out on the streets like so many other children. Her only possessions were a small sack and in it a bowl and spoon, along with something else, something she found in their room after they had taken her mother away, forgetting all about Rosie. That something was one well-worn shoe – her mother's.

Now wee Rosie had been on the streets for about six months when a shocked but thoughtful lady came across her late one night fast asleep in an Old Town close all on her own. And the lady took up the waif in her arms, and carried her to Dr Guthrie's small sanctuary and school in the Victoria Street church basement. And there Rosie was washed, her rags thrown away, and dressed in whatever clothes they had, and then fed. Wee Rosie was ravenous.

Of course Guthrie's first school was not a residential home like his later schools. But it did have a back room where a few victims of extreme neglect were sheltered on a temporary basis. So Rosie was there. But the volunteers there had a problem with Rosie. When she first arrived there clutching her small sack, she let them take it away, but not a little item that was in the sack wrapped in a dirty piece of linen – her mother's old shoe. When they tried gently to take it from her she nearly screamed the place down. And then she sobbed bitterly.

Well it was one of the local women who helped at the school that managed to calm down a tearful Rosie. She told the little girl that her shoe was filthy and that it would be given back to her when it as washed clean. Rosie then gave her helper the shoe and that was exactly what happened. Only when the shoe was given back to Rosie it looked a bit different. Two tiny cloth arms and legs had been attached to the shoe, and eyes, a nose, and a smiling mouth had been painted on the toe. For the first time since she had arrived, Rosie's sullen and tear-stained face lit up in a wonderful smile. And from then on they would often find Rosie talking to the shoe, scolding it, cuddling it, and laughing at it. She never went to bed without her shoe.

Considered a special case, Rosie was kept at the school until she was 13 years of age. She had grown tall for her age and pretty as well. She had been taught to read, write and count. And, as was the custom with Guthrie's children, a job was found for Rosie as a 'tweenie' – a kitchen maid – in a large house in the New Town. It was the home of a prominent musician and his family where every day Rosie heard beautiful music. On Sundays she went to church with the family, and soon she was singing in the church choir. For there was something special in Rosie's voice, something that had been noted.

By the time Rosie Gale was 18 she was singing at big church concerts. Then she became bolder and sang at a 'Free-and-Easy'. These were becoming popular in the Old Town, where any pub with a large backroom and a piano could recruit a master of ceremonies and hold a 'Free-and-Easy' concert on a Saturday night. While singing at one of these swallies, Rosie was approached by a theatrical agent who signed her up as a professional singer, billed not as Rosie gale but as Rosalind Nightingale. Soon she was performing in music halls and then concert halls. She even sang for the Empress Queen Victoria on one of her royal visits to Scotland.

As well as being a beautiful singer, Rosie was a beautiful young woman. She met and married a generous and wealthy man, and they went to live in a fine house in Buckingham Terrace in the New Town. They had two sons and a daughter, and the years passed on. Rosie was a widow and 90 years old when her time came to pass away. On her death bed she asked her daughter to bring her a small package which was hidden away in the bottom drawer of a fine Chippendale chest of drawers just across from where she lay in a stately bedroom.

The old package was tightly bound up with pink ribbon. No-one in the family had seen it before. Rosie asked her daughter to give her what was in the parcel. It was an old shoe, with tiny cloth arms and legs attached, and two eyes and a smiling mouth painted on the toe. Rosie reached out for the shoe, held it to her cheek, closed her eyes, and with a wistful sigh died.

Now if you go into the Museum of Childhood, don't be overwhelmed by the many fine 19th century toys that could only have been bought by the minority who could afford them. Look instead into the tall glass cabinet full of smaller toys, especially dolls – china dolls, cloth dolls and wooden dolls. This is where once you might have seen a tiny old shoe with tiny cloth arms and legs attached to it. The painted eyes and nose on the toe of the shoe would be almost worn away, the painted mouth gone. But it was there once and smiled up at wee Rosie Gale. And that is the story that was told to me by those who saw her and heard her sing.

> Beside John Knox House, the High Street narrows where once The Netherbow Port, principal gateway to Edinburgh stood. There are two old Netherbow Houses that survive – the Royal Goldsmith's House which survived because John Knox the Protestant reformer may have lived there during the final months of his life, and next door Moubray House where Daniel Defoe stayed as an English Government spy during the later Union crisis – two national crises and two controversial writers.
>
> The Netherbow is the perfect location for Scotland's Storytelling Centre, where John has often held sway. On the other side of the Netherbow, behind the High Street, is St Patrick's Church which was an important focus for the Old Town's Irish community. I remembered John leading an enthusiastic audience through a medley of humorous and sentimental Irish songs at a St Pat's fundraiser in the Storytelling Centre. There was not a dry eye in the house and the songs were delivered with immense skill and panache.

The Netherbow Port

John now wanted to see the Sedan Chair garage in Tweeddale Court, remembering Hamish and Malachi. This was also the location of an unsolved murder...

'What about the Netherbow Port, John?' I diverted.

'Everyone and everything came through here,' coaxed Stuart, camera at the ready.

'Well,' – the Fee eyes were glinting dangerously – 'why was the gate here in the first place?'

We were clearly not the people who were going to answer that question.

Story of a Head

Clearing out or cleaning up an old 'glory hole' or lumber room is usually a messy job – a job one keeps putting off; hardly an exciting or rewarding task though you might well find something unexpected, something long forgotten.

Now that was the way of it for two labourers given the job of cleaning up an old store room of what had once been a monastery in Richmond, Surrey, now the Duke of Suffolk's lodging. It was just an old storeroom cluttered with timber, broken furniture and other rubbish and rubble.

So our two menials, up to their knees in all this, must have felt some of sort excitement when they broke through a thick curtain of cobwebs to find what they thought at first was an old empty wooden coffin – except that it was not empty. As they dragged it out they saw that the lid was loose, improperly fastened and so a layer of dust had covered its contents – the figure of a man, but not a decomposed one. It was obviously a wax dummy or doll, they thought at first. But the sharper one of the two noted that the inside of the box was lined with lead and he knew what that meant. The box was indeed a coffin and the discovered waxen figure was an embalmed corpse. It must have been somebody at some time but it was a nobody now – obviously not fit for a tomb or even a humble grave.

In any case our two 'discoverers' were no respecters of persons except for those with power over them, and they had seen plenty of dead bodies in days of war and regular famines. The coarser one of the two became immediately intrigued by the head of the corpse, and his strong hands wrenched it from its body and held it up by its long dark reddish hair, tugged its beard and mocked it, throwing it then with a loud laugh to his companion who stood somewhat back from their gruesome find. The companion nonetheless caught the head and threw it back with an angry curse, then a nervous laugh. Horseplay with a nobody's head was, after all, a break from their grimy labours – a break, however, which was interrupted.

It was John Stow, an English chronicler, who came upon the scene accompanied by a visiting craftsman – Lancelot Young, the Master Glazier to the Queen Elizabeth of England. John Stow, by some way or another, knew the identity of the now desecrated corpse and enlightened his horrified companion who drove off the unthinking ghouls – for the moment anyway. He then knelt, lifted the head and, cradling it in his arm, smoothed its auburn hair and beard. Both hair and beard, though dry of all moisture, retained the savour of scent. So it was then that Lancelot Young took the head back with him to his home in Wood Street, London, where it appears he gave it some prominence of place and reverence.

According to the written testimony of chronicler John Stow, this head had once sat proudly on the broad shoulders of a man described by a contemporary as being neither tall or nor short but of medium height. Once the noblest head in Scotland, respected throughout that land and far beyond it for its wisdom, culture and learning, but also for its knowledge of fighting skills in an age when these were greatly valued. True it was a head that could never have worn a halo for the affairs of the heart – indeed the flesh had often overruled heart and head, though not without troubling the Christian conscience within for he wore a heavy belt of iron for his sins. But in happier times this head was so often raised to nod in acknowledgement the usual hurrahs and waves of High Street and Canongate people as its owner with a colourful entourage behind him. This head rode down those streets to inspect – with some pride – the building of a royal residence at Holyrood Abbey which one day would grow to be a palace for monarchs – the Stewart kings, of which he was surely the greatest and certainly the most respected. For the head in our story, rescued from desecration, and coveted by the master glazier to the Queen, was the head of Scotland's Renaissance prince, James IV of Scotland.

This was the king who, in September 1513, at the head of one of Scotland's biggest and best equipped armies, rode to disastrous defeat on the field of Flodden – a king in his prime, at 40 years of age, cut down like a flower in the field and with him the best and most promising of his nation's manhood. 10,000 of them fell within three hours of the battle – the 'Flowers of the Forest'. The battle over, his body was removed from a sea of dead, and despite its mutilation was identified by his friends and those of his victors who knew him, especially their leader, the Earl of Surrey.

So was the body of the slain king, disembowelled, embalmed, placed in a lead lined coffin and sent to London for the English Queen's instructions. Her husband, King Henry VIII, was at that time warring in France. But to cut a longer story short, plans for its ultimate destination were changed and, in the meantime, it found its way to the old monastery of Sheen in Richmond, Surrey, where our story begins. But then came the dissolution or the breaking up of monasteries throughout England, which was when the old building became lodgings for the Duke of Suffolk. And so it was that eventually the sexton of St. Michael's Churchyard in Wood Street buried the head in an anonymous grave. There was no stone or memorial to mark its site.

Even so, the biggest reminders of this king and his tragic end are here in Edinburgh itself, and made of solid stone. Disbelief was the first reaction of the Scots when they heard the awful news of that colossal defeat and great loss of life on the field of Flodden. It was a country stricken with grief for few homes were untouched by the tragedy. Then came fear, real fear, that there was more killing to come. Edinburgh was a city reeling with shock, its leadership was dead. But deputised authorities wasted no time for a follow-up was sure to come. All available men were ordered to arms and night watches organised. Lamenting women were told to get on with their weeping and wailing and praying, but elsewhere, not on the city streets, under pain of banishment. A new wall had to be built – and quickly! And sections of this great Flodden Wall that surrounded the city can be seen to this day. One large stretch can be seen from the top of St Mary's Street climbing the Pleasance. Here at the foot of the High Street, brass setts on the ground outline the site of its biggest fortified gate, the Netherbow Port.

The time for an official memorial was to come much later after that tragic event and I'm sure that James IV of Scotland – the 'Father of Scottish Chivalry' – would have approved.

FLODDEN 1513

To the Brave of Both Nations

But actually the largest memorial is on this spot in Scotland's capital where the effects of that battle were felt for generations to come.

> So now we went through that Netherbow Port or gateway into the church settlement of the Canons' Gait or Street, leading to Holyrood Abbey. At one time this was a different town, but its story is now woven into Edinburgh's. John never missed a beat, leaving us trailing along till he came to a halt near the head of the 'Gait' pointing up to a stone head above the houses.

> 'Edinburgh does have stories in which not every character ends up dead. Some are romantic, with people actually getting married at the end – like this one.'

Morocco Land

It happened during the reign of a king who rode down our Royal Mile, a colourful entourage behind him, to be crowned at Holyrood Abbey. A tumultuous welcome there was for Charles I, the whole population of the city turned out to greet him. But alas, his romance with Edinburgh, indeed with Scotland itself, like some of the other Stuarts before him, did not last all that long. His political and religious policies provoked much disturbance and opposition throughout the country, and nowhere more than in its capital where riots were endemic. The threat of mob rule turned its peaceful enough provost into a man determined to enforce law and order.

During one riot his own house was attacked, and the ringleader of that angry crowd was singled out as Andrew Gray – a young student with good social connections, but such things cut no ice with the furious provost. Whatever the young man's family and its gentry status, he was going to die! But first he was thrown into the city's dreadful High Street jail – the Tolbooth, already crowded with protesters, to be tried in two days time then hanged immediately afterwards, by order of the provost of Edinburgh.

But Andrew Gray's kinsfolk and influential friends were quick to act, with brandy for the turnkey, bribes and files, they sprang the young man from the Tolbooth Jail on the eve of his execution. In the pitch black of night, he was hurried down Mary King's Close in the High Street, rowed across the Nor' Loch to where a horse awaited him, then with great speed he rode through the sleeping village of Broughton down to the fishing village of Newhaven where a fishing boat was ready to sail at first light with himself on board. It was to land him on the Fife coast across the Forth, and there in Fife he was to stay with relatives until things in the city had calmed down. Perhaps he could then return. But that never happened.

It had all been well-planned except that the planners had forgotten that the king had not succeeded, as he had promised, in clearing the Forth of ruthless pirates – especially the Moorish pirates. They were a plague on its fishing fleets, destroying them, killing or sometimes carrying off their crews to North Africa. Back home they could sell a ship's crew for a good price in the slave markets of Morocco or Algiers. Dark-skinned they were and not to be trifled with – ferocious but skilful seamen in their strange flat-bottomed ships topped by red sails. They were the pride of the Emperor of Morocco, to whom they often gave a good share of their plunder of gold, silver, silks and precious stones. The Emperor loved his pirates – they were virtually his navy. And they were the reason why Andrew Gray never reached the Fife coast. In fact he vanished from Scotland altogether.

As for Scotland itself, the next ten years brought more disorder and then civil war throughout the land. Next came a plague worse than pirates, 'the Black Death' – the unstoppable bubonic plague, which carried off young and old alike as it did also in England, brought to our islands by rats escaping from in-coming sea vessels. Plagues and epidemics were no strangers to Scotland, but this outbreak was the worst ever. In 1646, in Edinburgh, it was recorded that there were scarcely 50 men able to defend the city.

So you can imagine the reaction of its demoralised provost when he received the news that a huge fleet of Moorish pirates had landed at the Port of Leith and were now heading for the capital. He had hardly gathered the remains of his Council together when the pirates reached their destination. The weary provost, armed like his small band of officials, watched them swarm up the deserted Canongate, approaching the Netherbow.

A motley crew indeed! Colourful if fearful looking, the Moors were not ragged, scruffy-looking pirates. They wore turbans and sleeveless tunics of silk, of every bright colour and shade. Their skins were a golden brown or ebony black. The people of Edinburgh could see the glitter of earrings and arm bracelets and the flash of steel, for these pirates were armed to the teeth. At their head was the leader, swarthy, scarred, and black bearded, his sword drawn as he swaggered up to the well-fortified Netherbow Port.

He glared through the wide grille of that gate at the provost, Sir John Smith, but never addressed him directly, speaking instead in his own Moorish tongue to the mixed-race Moor who stood at his side as his interpreter. And, as he spoke, it was curious how he kept turning his head left and right, up and down at the houses all around him, shaking his head as he did so. Then his interpreter, as he was bid, told the provost in English that he was to open the city gate immediately. But the provost, in pleading tones, answered back that as the city's leader he could not do that, and he explained that the city was rife with plague and that the pirates themselves would be in danger if they entered it. The pirate chief laughed loud and scornfully at this, oddly enough even before his interpreter translated it back to him in Moorish.

Now it was at that point that the wealthiest merchant in the city, Sir William Gray, took over negotiations from the despairing provost by offering the pirate a huge sum of gold and silver if he would go away and leave them to their own misery. The pirate chief, with a quizzical smile, nodded acceptance and through the gate his eyes followed Sir William hurrying up the High Street to gather the ransom, a street empty except for carts loaded with the dead victims of the plague being trundled off for burial.

Then the bags of gold and silver arrived and were lowered over the gate to the pirate chief who next staggered the Edinburgh official by demanding further that the provost's son also be handed over as a hostage. But the provost cried out in agony that he had no son, only a daughter – dying of the plague. As proof he had her carried down to the gate in a litter, weeping as he did so, his officials standing well back for fear of infection. And now the strangest thing of all occurred. The pirate chief looked down through the gate at the frail young woman lying on the litter, unconscious and ghostly white, save for the red plague sores that covered her once lovely face. Then he lowered his head in silence for a full minute.

A hush fell over the whole scene on either side of that gate. He then looked up and straight at the provost, and speaking now in the provost's own Scottish tongue, the Moorish pirate told him: 'Open the yet an haun her ower tae me. A hae Moorish doctors whause ancient medicines wark wonders. She will be cured. Ye will hae her back.' And, at the stunned disbelieving faces of the provost and his officials, he snapped angrily, 'In yer hauns she will dee. Gin she dies in oor hauns, ye cin tak back aw yer gowd an yer siller!'

So the young sick woman was passed gently through a narrow opening of the great gate to the pirates who then carried her to a house close by in the Canongate, which was empty like so many others because of the plague. It was there that the Moorish doctors began to treat her with medicines unknown to the Western world. Within only three days, all those wretched rings of red sores on her face and body had gone. On the fourth day, Mary, for that was her name, rose from her sick bed, weak but cured. The pirate chief handed her back to her father who was mystified like all the others by this fearsome, yet now caring Moorish pirate, who spoke Scots with an unmistakable Edinburgh accent, and now revealed his true identity.

He told them that he was brown of complexion because of 10 years sailing some of the hottest seas in the world. He was no Moor – his name was Andrew Gray, born and bred in Edinburgh. As a student he had escaped hanging for his part in a riot, only to be captured at sea by Moorish pirates. He was to be taken to Morocco and sold there with the captured ship's crew. But then that pirate ship had nearly perished in a North Sea storm, and he had struggled with the Moors to save their ship, really to save his own life. The pirate captain of the ship had only praise and gratitude for his brave efforts, which then turned to admiration when he watched the young man fight off the Spanish pirates who tried to destroy their Moorish rivals. 'What else could I do?' he said. 'Be killed by the Spaniards?'

So when the ship got back to Morocco, Andrew Gray was not sold in any slave-market for its captain took him on as a member of his crew. He sailed the seven seas as a pirate. Better, he said, than being worked to death as a slave. The years went by, he was now a fully grown man in command of his own ship – fame and fortune had followed. Then the Emperor of Morocco made him an admiral of a whole fleet of ships. Yet, throughout those swashbuckling years, he never ceased to long for the chance to wreak revenge on his own city of Edinburgh and its provost.

Now the Emperor knew his story too well and eventually gave him permission to sail his fleet there, plunder the city and destroy it with fire and sword. Well, said Andrew Gray to his astounded listeners, 'You know the rest. I am going now and you will never see me again. You can keep your silver and your gold. My good Moorish doctors have been around the city; they tell me that your plague is coming to an end, but they will leave you a chest with their ancient medicines – the Moors are a clever people. So Farewell!' he said. But before he turned to go, the provost's beautiful daughter Mary walked to his side and openly declared her love for him and her wish to leave with him. He was visibly moved for he loved her too, he had never left her sick bed, day or night. Her father, the provost, was speechless and bewildered.

So in the end, Andrew Gray, did not go back to Morocco, but sent back his fleet of ships with a message of regret and gratitude for the Emperor. As the Moorish pirates sailed out of Leith harbour they beat out on their African drums a tattoo of sad farewell to their leader who watched, with some feeling, the red sails of their ships disappear into the grey mists of the Firth of Forth. Then the pirate chief renounced his former life and married the provost's daughter. Mind you, the house they went to live in was not in Edinburgh – perhaps Andrew Gray still had that thing about the city – but outside the Netherbow Gate in the

Canongate, which was a town in its own right at that time. In fact, it was the very house in which Mary had been nursed back to health. Nor did Andrew Gray ever forget the Emperor of Morocco for he had his effigy sculpted in stone above its close entrance – a half-figure with a turbaned head, earrings, a necklace of beads and arm-bracelets, and below it, a shield with a coat of arms said to have been a mix of the family of the Smiths and the Grays.

The effigy and shield, though well-worn, are still here today and the name of Gray is listed among the earliest owners of this close. This is perhaps enough to suggest that the story just told is more than an old wives' tale. It certainly fits Sir Walter Scott's description of the Edinburgh of his time as 'Mine Own Romantic Town'. But there is nothing romantic about the close heading below the emperor's effigy today. It reads 'Mid-Common Close'. When I was a boy, it read 'Morocco Land'.

'Scott knew the Canongate well himself, did he not, John? Several of his stories were set here.'

'Chronicles of the Canongate,' purred John appreciatively.

'He was an old Tory,' grumbled Stuart.

'Which couldn't be said of another writer who drew some inspiration from this place,' John countered.

'Do you mean Robert Fergusson?' asked Stuart.

'And buried here, but I mean Charles Dickens.'

Before we could collect our thoughts, John was ushering us through the pend at Moray House into St John's Street.

Dickens in The Canongate

It has been said that old stones are full of stories and we should let them speak for themselves. Now the Canongate is full of old stones and full of stories, and no-one knew that better than our own Walter Scott, a great listener and collector of stories. There were tales he learned from the old stone structures and ruins he was forever inspecting, and also stories he was told by folk who lived around them. Most of these narratives were to find their way into the famous historical novels and other works that made him 'The Wizard of the North'. Yet I often wonder if he missed out one story, though the one I'm thinking about is a story of small account, a minor issue, more likely a topic for local gossip which it certainly would be at that time, in the later 18th century.

However, it was left to another great storyteller and writer to make the most of that minor matter – Charles Dickens, all the way up from his own city of stories, London. But that would have meant that the great man himself would have to have been down the Canongate, at least up here in Edinburgh. Now I thought at first that this would have been unlikely. But to my surprise, Charles Dickens had indeed been up in Edinburgh and more than once too, fishing for stories. His first recorded visit was in 1834 when he was here as a young newspaper reporter for *The Times*, covering a retirement dinner in honour of the eminent statesman Lord Grey, who was receiving the Freedom of the City. A most efficient, sharp-eyed and eared reporter was Charles. He seldom missed a trick.

Then seven years later in 1841 he was back, and this time he himself was receiving the Freedom of the City as a popular and distinguished author, and socialising with the 'Big Wigs'. Edinburgh was all about lawyers then. It still is. He became particularly friendly with two judges, Lord Jeffrey and Lord Cockburn, who were both pioneers in Old Town Conservation and had streets named after them. Yet Dickens had a more personal connection with the City, for his wife Kate spoke with a broad Scots accent like her father, George Hogarth, an Edinburgh man. On his third visit in 1858, Dickens concluded his speech to a distinguished gathering with the words: 'Coming back to Edinburgh is like coming home'.

But to get nearer to the Canongate story, we have to remember that, by this time, Dickens' now personal friend Lord Jeffrey, had taken the English author on sight-seeing tours, certainly to Abbotsford, the country home of Sir Walter Scott for whom Charles had enormous respect and admiration. He did not however admire the new-looking monument to Scott in Princes Street. He said it was like the spire of a Gothic church just lopped off and stuck in the ground. Lord Jeffrey, no doubt, would have whisked him away and down the city's great historic highway, a Royal Mile of which he himself was so proud – the Lawnmarket, the High Street, and the Canongate.

Jeffrey knew these streets like the back of his hand, every close and wynd, and the stories associated with them. On this visit to Edinburgh, Dickens had, at a city banquet, quoted from 'A Man's a Man for A' That', so his distinguished guide would have him led off the Canongate here through St John's Close into St John's Street. There he would have beheld the oldest Masonic lodge in the world, as it is claimed – the Kilwinning Lodge, where Robert Burns had been honoured as its Poet Laureate in 1787. To the right of that was Lord Monbodo's mansion where the eccentric literary old judge used to entertain the great and good of Edinburgh's 'Golden Age' – the literati, the clever people, and the rich people, for they all lived around there anyway.

St John's was a street of distinction, which the aristocrats and the gentry only left when the New Town was ready for them, people like Lord Wemyss. He once lived there, Jeffrey told Dickens, in that old mansion next to the Kilwinning Lodge. Another of the Wemyss family lived in the old mansion nearer the end of the street, that large house with the overgrown garden and shuttered windows. Nobody of importance lives there now, not after she died, a sad case by all accounts, Dickens would have been told. Enough said! But the ears of the ex-reporter would have pricked up, catching the scent of a story. A sad case? Who was she, this relative of Lord Wemyss, and what happened to her?

'Well, she was the beautiful young Lady Betty,' Jeffrey told him, 'Lady Elizabeth Charteris, living there towards the end of the last century. She fell in love and was slighted. Her groom didn't turn up on the wedding day. In her stricken state, she retired to her house there to live alone and never left it until she died 26 years later, and except for local gossip there is no more to be said.'

Now Dickens, as we all know, based many of his characters on real people and incidents. So who was he thinking about some years later when he was writing one of his finest novels and describing a bitter old lady living in a large house with an overgrown garden? She had, he described, lived there behind closed curtains for more than 20 years. This lady had been slighted when young, rejected in love, and condemned herself to the life of a vengeful recluse. To my knowledge, our author never revealed the source of this character's inspiration. All I know is that as a reader of his stories, whenever I read *Great Expectations* and come to Miss Havisham, I cannot help thinking about Lady Betty Charteris, and that old house here in St John's Street off the Canongate.

For a moment we all seemed to see that decaying shuttered old house, but John had an unexpected addendum.

'And that's not all. Another time Dickens' eye was caught by a gravestone in Canongate Kirkyard. "Ebenezeer Scroggie, Mealman" was the faded inscription. But Dickens read it as "Meanman", which got Charles thinking about the annual Christmas story he still had to write.'

'So Scrooge was born in the Canongate?'

That was too obvious a question for John and it lay unanswered, as he proceeded back to the Mile, and down to the heart of the Canongate with its Mercat Cross, its Kirkyard with Robert Fergusson's grave, and its venerable Tolbooth, flanked to the south by the Museum of Edinburgh and the Scottish Poetry Library. Everywhere we looked, the stag with a cross between its antlers, symbol of the Canongate, appeared in stone, and above the church facade in shining gold.

John, as ever, obliged, with the background story, though with a personal touch of knowledge from his own continuing Roman Catholic tradition.

'The legend of the stag takes us back to the early 12th century during the reign of David I. David was a warrior king, but also a very

religious one; his mother was Queen Margaret who became
St Margaret.

'David had just attended mass in the castle on the feast day of the
Exaltation of the Holy Cross on 14 September. Now, after mass, and
against the advice of the monks who served the castle, David went on
a hunting trip with his nobles into the Drumselch forest below Arthur's
Seat. There that he got separated from his nobles and was attacked by
a great stag. The stag unhorsed him and then charged him as he lay
on the ground. In sheer desperation he thrust out his arm, gripped its
front antler and gasped with disbelief when it turned into a rood or
cross. Then with a great roar the stag ran off.

'The king's nobles soon found him, lying unconscious, and took
him back to the castle; and that night in a dream he heard a voice
calling to him three times to build an abbey for the canons. And in
1128 he founded the abbey which was built right where he'd met the
stag. And Holyrood Abbey is there to this day, within the palace of
Holyroodhouse. When it was built, David often stayed there, and in
those days since people liked to live near the king, they began to build

their houses, more and more of them stretching up the hill. So a new town or burgh was born and granted by a royal charter in the 1140s.

'As to its name, it was called the Canongate, nothing to do with cannons but to do with canons or monks who were walking about their business. Now, to the Scots, a walk or street was a gait, so the new burgh came to be called the Canongate. And the Canongate remained a small town or burgh in its own right. It had its own council and coat of arms, the stag's head, above its own tollbooth.'

'The Canongate wasn't just about the rich and famous though?' prompted Stuart. 'Not after those and such as those moved to their big houses in the New Town.'

Like every question we had asked on this walk so far, John took this as a cue for something he already wanted to explore. But he seemed especially pleased with Stuart's question. His mouth stayed serious, giving nothing away, but there was a glint, almost a twinkle in the eyes.

'This way then, lads, and we'll find out,' and John led us over the street into Bakehouse Close behind the Museum of Edinburgh.

The Canongate Butcher

Well, I suppose you could call this a story though you would have to call it a true one. But then, as you know, my stories are all true. It's a short story though that concerns this close, a Canongate butcher's shop and a wee Canongate lassie. The Close is still here, the butcher's shop has long gone and so has the wee lassie though she far outlived the butcher. It's a story that begins in the early 1850s, a bad time for the Canongate. The people of substance, position and wealth, had long left it to live in the beautiful and spacious streets of Edinburgh's New Town. And with the building of the new road beneath Calton Hill, the Old Canongate was no longer the main eastern approach to the city.

Nevertheless, the Canongate was becoming more and more a place to
live for the ever increasing number of people who continued to flood
the city during that century. These were the country folk displaced by
agricultural innovation still ongoing. There were also people from the
north, displaced by the break-up of the clan system following the
failure of the 1745 Rebellion and the consequent 'Clearances'. Then
there were the continuing 'Irish Invasions' – people escaping poverty
and persecution in their own land. And all this movement added up to
a desperate demand for basic shelter and sustenance, a demand that
was met in part by the new owners of the worthy old houses that the
well-to-do had left behind. So a growing landlord class divided and
sub-divided these old houses to pack into them as many of the poor as
could just manage to pay the rents.

A good example of this situation in the mid-19th century Canongate,
was Bakehouse Close. Sir Archibald Acheson had long left his mansion
to the east; the prosperous incorporations of the Hammermen and then
the Bakers had gone from their properties to the west. By 1851, 230

people were recorded as living in this ancient and tiny close – perhaps surviving is the better word. By 1871, there were 250 of them. And among those crowded poor of the Canongate at that time, Helen McKay, the wee girl in our story, was just waiting to be born, and born she was and a survivor alright! She grew up, married a Canongate man, brought up a family and was a very old lady by 1940 which was when she died.

I can remember her sitting by the fire in her then West Port attic home, smoking a clay pipe and talking of her Canongate days, when the only alternative to living in places like Bakehouse Close was the big house that stood in the wynd almost opposite the close – the Tolbooth Wynd. She called it the 'Pares Hoose', the house that Canongate folk lived in fear of – the Charity House of the Canongate. It was, of course, one of the City's three workhouses – the smallest and the most notorious! It is recorded that many a Canongate pauper collecting his small allowance was threatened with that house, and some preferred the street and starvation to living within its locked doors. It became a subject of an official enquiry. But the word 'starvation' brings us to the third feature in our story – the butcher's shop, just up from Bakehouse Close.

Now good fresh meat was not part of the staple diet of the Canongate poor for obvious reasons. Nevertheless, at least once a week they queued up outside that butcher's shop carrying bowls, tins and tureens, and all because of the young man, the butcher's nephew, who was serving his apprenticeship in his uncle's shop – Young John, they called him, to distinguish him from his uncle, Old John. He was a country lad hailing from the Midlothian village of Roslin and the hungry neighbours were queuing up for what they called his 'soup'. But it was never really soup in the proper sense of the word. The young butcher, after two or three days selling meat to the Old Town's more prosperous customers, would collect the numerous scraps left over after the cutting and, in his own time, would then boil them up into a rich brown liquid and this was what his poorer customers, with their pots and pans, were queuing up for.

And they were sorry when young John's apprenticeship was served and he went off to work in a shop in the Southside where, of course, his concoction was equally welcomed by the less than wealthy Southsiders. But not for long, for the young butcher was soon off to Canada, Montreal in fact, and there he experimented further with his product. His break was soon to come. France had been badly beaten in the Franco-Prussian war, and starvation followed its surrender. French Government agents in Montreal offered the young butcher a contract to supply his nutritious product, which he gladly accepted. Then it was back to Britain, London this time, where he produced an improved version of his magic liquid in a drink form, and from then on there was no stopping John Lawson Johnson. By this time he had found a name for his perfected product, two Latin words joined up – 'Bo' meaning 'ox', and 'vril' meaning 'life force'. This was the birth of Bovril!

The one-time Canongate butcher became a millionaire and went off to join all the other millionaires in the South of France, Cannes I believe, where he died in 1900. But not before he had paid many visits to his old village of Roslin, presenting generous donations including children's playground equipment and a cup for the Roslin bowlers to play for – the Bovril Cup. It is not known if John Lawson Johnson ever paid a visit to the Old Canongate, but when I stop with a party of tourists at Bakehouse Close and comment on its architecture, reeling off all the important people who once lived there, all the time I am thinking of the 250 people it once sheltered, and of the butcher's shop and the 'Pares House' or workhouse. And of young Helen McKay and her family who were lucky to escape it for, as you may have already guessed, Helen McKay was my Granny.

From Bakehouse Close on to Holyrood, we pass a range of historic buildings mixed in with some more recent additions, not least the Scottish Parliament. That turned John's mind in another direction, being an active campaigner for keeping the older fabric alive.

'Well I'm not about to give a lecture on the Old Town, the uniqueness of its structure and architecture.'

Stuart and I exchanged a look.

'People come from all over the world, go on tours of the Royal Mile with its old closes, buildings and houses, and hear their histories. It's all there for them. But it needn't have been, for in the past our Town Council often decided that in the name of progress parts of the Old Town must be demolished. Of course it is true that some old tenements were ready to collapse anyway but not them all. Some that were worth conserving were demolished. And it's still happening.'

'Caltongate development, right beside us' added Stuart.

'At least there's an argument about it,' I qualified, 'We owe a lot to Patrick Geddes, and Lord Cockburn before that I suppose.'

'The Conservationists, Donald, but they weren't the first. We have to remember Claudero.'

We both gave John a blank look.

The Conservationist

He was not an establishment figure and certainly not a person of means or influence. He did not even come from Edinburgh, but when he came to live in Edinburgh in the early 18th century, he fell in love with it till he died here 30 years later in 1789. His name was James Wilson and when he came from Cumbernauld to Edinburgh he brought with him a razor-sharp wit and an exceptional talent for insulting people, particularly those in authority or of high social standing.

 Wilson could write and appears to have been the sole voice protesting against the Council's mania for demolishing things. His protests took the form of a series of poems which were eventually published as 'Miscellanies in Prose and Verse' (1776) under the pen name of Claudero.

Just one example illustrates Claudero's unique way of making his point. We are about to approach Holyrood Palace from a short street, the Abbey Strand. But in Claudero's time the entrance was through a stately long porch built by the founder of the palace, James IV. Claudero stood helplessly watching it being pulled down for being 'an obstruction to traffic'. Then he went home and wrote his poem titled 'The Echo of the Royal Porch of the Palace of Holyrood which fell under military execution, Anno Domine 1753'. And, since the military guard at the palace were given the job of demolition, the soldiers became the prime target for his slicing satire:

'They do not deal in blood; nor yet in breaking human bones,
For Quixote-like they knock down stones;
Regardless they their mattocks ply to sort out Scots Antiquity.'
The ancient porch cries out in tears:
What is my crime, what is my blot?
Auld Reekie cried, 'Thou'st an old Scot.'

Three years later the next to go was the Mercat Cross, not the one we saw today beside the west side of St Giles, which was built in 1885, but one much older going back centuries when it was the centre of all official communication – royal pronouncements, declarations, and edicts. It was also a place of public executions. It stood a bit further down the High Street and by this time had become the city's meeting place for its traders, business men and lawyers. So when it was demolished in 1756 its loss was felt, until the council built a more modern facility for these important citizens – the Royal Exchange. But the fine new building was ignored for they continued to meet in the street, so it then became the City Chambers you know today. But to the Council, the famous old cross was yet another traffic obstruction. So tradition gave way to 'progress' and down it came, prompting Claudero's poem entitled 'The last speech and dying words of the cross which was hanged, drawn and quartered on Monday the 15th of March 1756 for the horrid crime of being an encumbrance to the street'.

I was built up in Gothic times
And have stood several hundred reigns.
Heavens, earth, and seas, all in a rage,
Like me will perish for 'Exchange'.

Then it was the turn of the great Netherbow Gate, and down it came, followed by Claudero's poem titled 'Sermon on the Condemnation of

the Netherbow Port', a really vitriolic piece castigating those
responsible. Of course in Claudero's time the decisions to demolish
objects of antiquity were never preceded by public consultation, so his
protests could only come after the damage was done. Yet James Wilson
pointed the way for others of like mind who came after him. His
immediate successor was Dr Patrick Neil whose 1829 pamphlet saved
the sole surviving corner of the Flodden Wall which the Council had
doomed as a 'useless encumbrance'. John Knox House was also lucky
when the combined efforts of the Society of Antiquaries and the newly
formed Free Church of Scotland saved it and, in the process, Moubray
House next door.

So Claudero was the man who spoke up for, and through stones. Yet
this fascinating character had a less commendable side to his writings.
All I can say in his defence is that Claudero's pen did not make him a
rich man, or a popular one as far as the people who counted in the city
were concerned. The well-kent figure in a shabby coat and cocked hat,
limping along with a crutch and dragging a lame foot behind him, had
a touch of 'Long John Silver', something of the darker side. His sharp

wit could become a deadly weapon when it came to lampooning and ridiculing an enemy, or someone else's enemy.

Someone might hold a grudge against someone but be powerless to hit back. But the aggrieved party could consult Claudero in one of his many drinking dens, brief him against his enemy, and for the sum of half a crown Claudero would produce a pamphlet dripping with ridicule and bile – a character assassination. This was then circulated round to the squirming dismay of its target. When short of custom, the bold Claudero was known to call on some successful citizen with a skeleton in his cupboard – some dubious circumstance in the origin of his acquired wealth or status. Then the satirist would hand his potential victim a masterful denunciation of his character and background, hilarious but deadly, and offer it to him for sale. A mere guinea or two would suffice, or perhaps Claudero could make much more selling it round the neighbourhood as a pamphlet. Of course it was purchased immediately and then destroyed, which is why so few of James Wilson's unofficial writings have survived.

But much of Claudero's work did survive, not least his predictions. For when it came to Edinburgh's future, James Wilson was a kind of Nostradamus of his time. Dying in the year of the French Revolution, though, he did not live to see many of his predictions come true. He foresaw the extension of the city as far as Portobello, a townscape with ordered beautiful streets that was a New Town, the absorption of Leith into Edinburgh, and the building of Granton Harbour. He prophesied that Edinburgh would become a world famous metropolis.

And finally, for all his powers of ridiculing other people, Claudero's greatest talent was for laughing at himself. He was known for telling many a story against himself, for his own amusement and that of others. It is typical of him, therefore, that, realising his only book-length work would have plenty of critics, he prefaced it by saying, 'Men's works in general resemble themselves; if these poems are lame, so is their author – Claudero.'

> By this time we were into the Abbey Strand, trying to imagine the covered walkway Claudero had lamented. Stuart was busy photographing the 16th century houses, and the wonderful sculptured unicorn from the royal arms of James v.
>
> John was in the middle of the road, commanding the approach from the Canongate, a diminutive yet authoritative figure, pork pie hat firmly angled above the steady gaze through large black framed spectacles, his eyes inquiring, receptive yet challenging, ironic and compassionate at once, with that ever ready glint of humour. Hardly a Claudero, but perhaps a latter-day Quixote gallantly recounting the tales of his favourite heroes, however neglected or humble, because they were part of this place and community.
>
> He was waiting patiently to resume his own account of Holyrood Abbey and its significance for the people of Edinburgh.

Abbey Strand Houses

Well, as you see, it once led directly to Holyrood Abbey built in the 12th century before there was a Holyrood Palace, which began as a guest house attached to the Abbey. There was an ancient right of sanctuary here until that right passed from the church to kings. It was then that Holyrood Palace, its grounds, indeed much of the Holyrood Park that you see today, were all designated as places of royal sanctuary – within these, a fugitive was safe. But by then the Abbey Sanctuary only offered refuge to those who were being pursued by creditors, who could otherwise have them thrown into jail for failing to pay their debts.

The debtor occupants in the Abbey Sanctuary were not the common people or the poor of the Old Town – to whom nobody would lend money anyway – they were the middling or genteel classes, or well-bred spendthrifts down on their luck. If they could escape their creditors to Holyrood and its sanctuary houses here in the Strand then they were spared imprisonment in the Tolbooth Jail. From all accounts, living conditions for the occupants of the Abbey Sanctuary were far superior to most of the Old Town population living in its wynds and closes. But they had to pay for their bed and board. Indeed, before they could enter the sanctuary they had to pay 20 shillings to the sanctuary superior, called the Baron Bailie. Thereafter they had to pay for rent and food which was actually higher in price than outside.

It would be true to say that they had all seen better days, the educated and cultured among them, and now and again a smattering of minor aristocrats – referred to as the 'Abbey Lairds' – whose very existence their creditors outside resented. These were angry, frustrated men whose appeals to the city courts were useless, and they gnashed their teeth especially on Sundays when their debtors were allowed to leave the sanctuary to visit relatives or friends in the city without fear of being molested by their creditors. It was their one privilege – they were free for 24 hours, from Saturday midnight to Sunday midnight when they must be back within the sanctuary boundary, else they were considered fair game for creditors on the look-out for them outside the sanctuary.

If a debtor was caught by a creditor outside the sanctuary after midnight on Sunday, then he or she came under the city's jurisdiction and ended up in the Tolbooth for non-payment of debt. This sort of cat-and-mouse situation led to incidents in which creditors were known to employ all kinds of stratagems to ensnare their debtors. One obviously trusting debtor accepted an invitation to an evening meal at the house of his creditor, who knew that his expected guest had privately disposed of his assets before entering the sanctuary. The purpose of this get-together was to discuss a deal that might satisfy them both. Of course this meeting could only be on the privileged Sunday and so it took place. A splendid evening it was too. A scrumptious supper, the best of wine, and the host couldn't have been more agreeable. He even pointed out to his guest the time on his clock – it was 11.30pm. He reminded him that he must be back at the sanctuary by midnight, and since a deal had been done it would be best if he hurried off home. But as the unsuspecting debtor was leaving he was met outside the door by a court-messenger with a court order and escorted to the Tolbooth – the real time was 12.30am. Putting back their clocks was a well-known ruse of wily creditors.

A much sought-after debtor – I think his name was Simon Sales – owed money to a group of building contractors who lived for the day when they could get their hands on him. And that day came. It was one privileged Sunday evening that Simon visited a friend who lived at the top of the Canongate. Other friends turned up too. The wine and ale flowed freely, so freely that Simon, including his friends, forgot all about the Sanctuary deadline, and it was well after midnight when they remembered. Simon was reminded about creditors' agents often on the prowl at that time of night and was persuaded to stay the night at his friend's, and could return to the sanctuary the next morning – in disguise of course. And that is exactly what Simon did, or tried to.

Alas, he was spotted halfway down the Canongate by prowlers in the pay of his creditors; the rate at which he was walking had attracted their attention. And now he was running for all he was worth, his pursuers hot on his heels. A tremendous race that ended when the breathless debtor threw himself across the sanctuary boundary line, but they were on him as he lay prostrate on the cobbles trying to drag him back by the legs over the line into the Canongate. It was then that a fierce tug-o-war took place, for Simon's fellow debtors now aware of what was going on just outside the sanctuary rushed out, grabbed him by the head and shoulders, and were trying to pull him back over the boundary line.

The tug-o-war ended when the Baron Bailie of the sanctuary arrived at the scene and ordered a cessation of hostilities and both sides to stand back from Simon lying there across the boundary line. He then, with great care, examined the position of the prostrate debtor and then announced his findings. He declared aloud to all and sundry that since the essential parts of the debtor – his head and upper body, lay within the sanctuary then he belonged to its community, where upon the Abbey Lairds carried Simon shoulder high in triumph back into the Sanctuary House.

Another witness to what it was like to live in the sanctuary was the noted English essayist Thomas de Quincey. He would know alright for he was one of its occupants. The writer, it seems, had just been paying a visit to Edinburgh but stayed instead for 30 years and wrote several works during that period. But he was also an opium addict, an indulgence which he could ill afford and so resorted to borrowing, his main creditors being landladies and opium sellers from whom he sought refuge in the Abbey Sanctuary. De Quincey described some of its occupants as exotic, intelligent, cultured or eccentric, and we have already seen how supportive of each other they could be.

But this haven ended in 1880 when imprisonment for debt was abolished, though the original Sanctuary House remains here just outside the gates of Holyrood Palace. Its boundary, once called the 'Sanctuary Girth', is now lined with those brass embedded cobbles, each marked with an 'S'. There to remind us of an Old Town tradition that existed from the time of the Abbey's foundation in 1128.

> We had reached the Palace of Holyroodhouse, the very end of the Royal Mile with all it component parts – Castlehill, Lawnmarket, Tron, Netherbow, Canongate and Abbey Strand. But John had a last card up his sleeve, leading us over to the forecourt of the Scottish Parliament where the grounds run out into Holyrood Park.
>
> Was something political brewing, or perhaps a poem, even a song from all the Scottish verses inscribed on the Parliament's Canongate wall?
>
> 'Was there ever a time when here was no such thing as entertainment, anywhere in the world? A time when people were solely occupied with just staying alive?'
>
> 'Some situations maybe...'
>
> 'Even in a siege though – the arts in Sarajevo. Even in Auschwitz...'
>
> 'Aye, the grimmer the situation, the more need for it,' pounced John, 'and our earliest people, the poorest in medieval Scotland knew how to make their own entertainment.'

Robin Hood in Edinburgh

Now, unlike the kings, the nobility and the bishops, the common folk of Edinburgh could not sit back in their palaces or mansions and pay singers, dancers and actors to perform for them on specially built stages. But the poor had their entertainers nonetheless, travelling from one town or village to another – street artists and performers, now as popular as ever in our own Fringe Festival.

But in those times there were also seasonal celebrations that reached back into pre-Christian days, pagan and Celtic traditions which the early church wisely absorbed into its culture. They are still with us as Easter, May Day, Hallowe'en, Christmas or Yule, and Hogmanay. These became holy days, and so holidays, along with festivals or feast days celebrating an individual saint. The words certainly suggest that some enjoyment was involved, something to set against the drabber round of existence, the ever present threats of war, famine, disease and death.

During these festivals the Church often staged its own dramas, the Mystery Plays, involving the community in the enacting of Bible stories, or processions and rituals marking the acts of a local saint such as St Giles. But there were even older rituals such as the May Day Games, opening with the crowning of a 'Queen of the May' here on Arthur's Seat, the cutting of fresh boughs for circle dances, and washing in the dew. And the night before a great bonfire was lit on Calton Hill, and spaces were set out on Greenside and in the High Street for the revels. An 'Abbot of Unreason' was appointed to lead the fun, for as the title suggests some licence was involved, some anarchy to be loosed.

Crowd participation was the order of the day – the opportunity for a hard-pressed population to let their hair down, forget their worries and enjoy themselves. Men, women and children were expected to dress up in outlandish ways, as carnival mummers, and they did with gusto. They could also take part in mock battles that were fought at Greenside, remembering popular heroes and saints, not all of them Scottish. You could see St George chasing a dragon snorting real fire – so realistic that the children cheered when the dragon was slain.

Another favourite hero, the star turn of the day, was a 12th century English outlaw, a man of the Greenwood, and so of May Day, Robin Hood. His crowd appeal was not hard to explain, as he drove off the

Sherriff of Nottingham's henchmen. Robin had fed the poor, after of course robbing the rich with the help of his Merry Men such as Little John, Friar Tuck, Will Scarlett, not to forget the lovely Maid Marian, who was nonetheless played by a man in a blonde wig.

But the popularity of Robin Hood and his band of outlaws was put to severe test on the May Day of 1558, at a time when the struggle between Catholic and Protestant ideas was becoming fiercer. There was pressure on all sides to tighten up the social order and the May Day celebrations with their rowdy fun and games came under thorough scrutiny. The Church authorities had never been too happy about this Robin Hood and his Merry Men business. Perhaps it was thought that the merrymaking was becoming a bit too merry and so a bad example was being shown to the participating crowds. Besides, Robin Hood had been an outlaw defying the authorities of his time, not to mention the fact that his antics were often performed on a Sunday – the 'Sabbath'. So by public statute, the play was banned. But the city magistrates had not been enforcing the law and the play had gone on just the same.

Now May had come round again, despite all the political disputes and religious controversy, and the festival was ready to begin in the normal way. As was customary the principal characters in the play – Robin Hood, Little John, Friar Tuck, the Sheriff of Nottingham and Maid Marian, with all the supporting cast – had been picked from members of the community. Having gone early as usual to Holyrood Park to cut fresh green boughs, people were re-entering the town through the Netherbow Port. A large and lively crowd had already gathered, too lively for the watchful representatives of authority. This was the moment to act according to plan and statute.

The law enforcers, the slightly hapless Town Guard, reinforced on this occasion by some hardier men-at-arms, were given the signal to carry out their orders and stop the play. Pandemonium ensued. The crowd went crazy. Riots spread throughout the Old Town. People and properties were attacked. Some rioters were arrested and imprisoned in the Tolbooth, where the city magistrates had taken refuge in fear of their lives. One of the ringleaders, a shoemaker called Kylton was sentenced to immediate hanging, and that was when things got worse. The mob broke into the Jail, freeing not only Kylton but all the other prisoners as well. Then they smashed the gibbet, hauled out the cowering magistrates from their hiding places, and forced them forces them to proclaim an indemnity for all rioters who laid down their arms. All this for love of Robin Hood and his Merry Men. And reprisals followed in due course with arrests, floggings, cropping of ears and long spells in the stocks where the rebels had time to reflect on their defiance.

Yet some 30 years later, the now Protestant Kirk's General Assembly was still complaining and protesting about the profaning of the Sabbath by the Robin Hood plays. But gradually the increasing power of the Church and its influence over communities did bring about the end of the popular plays, though not the celebration of May Day. That continued out there in the valleys of Arthur's Seat, away from the view of magistrates and ministers alike. And it continues today, with renewed vigour, here and on Calton Hill.

As for Robin Hood and his Merry Men, they live on too. For all the world needs heroes to stand up against powerful and oppressive authority, in the name of justice and the commonweal. We need heroes, well and lesser known, along with the stories that keep them alive, and the entertainment that keeps us living and not merely existing. So don't forget the stories, because, good friends, when the stories are forgotten then so are the people.

So that was the end of our walk, a fitting conclusion, but not of our talk. Since, as with all good storytelling, it was the beginning not the end of the conversation. We repaired together to what was once Lucky Spence's ale house in the Canongate, a favoured haunt of debtors, merrymakers, and storytellers, to salute our guide.

To John Fee! Storyteller of Edinburgh. For his name is inscribed in the book of life as one who loves humanity, not least the people of this special place, the Old Town, our city's still beating heart.

Share, explore, experience and celebrate our storytelling heritage.

0131 556 9579

The **Scottish Storytelling Centre** is the home of Scotland's stories on Edinburgh's picturesque Royal Mile. The Centre presents a seasonal programme of storytelling, theatre, dance, music and literature, supported by exciting visual arts, craft and multimedia exhibitions. The Centre also hosts the **Scottish International Storytelling Festival** in October, which is a highlight of Scotland's autumn.

You've seen the landscape, vibrant cities and historic buildings, now experience the magic of live stories and feed your imagination. Don't miss out on the warmth and energy of modern culture inspired by tradition!

www.scottishstorytellingcentre.co.uk

Some other books published by **LUATH** PRESS

Calton Hill: Journeys and Evocations

Stuart McHardy and Donald Smith
ISBN: 978-1-908373-85-4 PBK £7.99

 Experience the scenery
and folklore of
Edinburgh's iconic
Calton Hill through new
eyes in the second
instalment in McHardy
and Smith's Journeys and Evocations
series. This blend of prose, poetry,
photography and history is the
perfect gift for any visitor to
Scotland's capital city.

*McHardy is driven by a passion for
making connections. His vision is of an
interconnected, inter-related environment.
His values are those of a cultural ecologist,
storyteller as well as researcher, poet as
well as scholar. He sets out to illuminate
and to persuade.*
CENCRASTUS

Arthur's Seat: Journeys and Evocations

Stuart McHardy and Donald Smith
ISBN: 978-1-908373-46-5 PBK £7.99

 Arthur's Seat, rising
high above the
Edinburgh skyline, is
the city's most awe-
inspiring landmark.
Although thousands
climb to the summit every year, its
history remains a mystery, shrouded in
myth and legend.

The first book of its kind, *Arthur's Seat:
Journeys and Evocations* is a salute to
the ancient tradition of storytelling,
guiding the reader around Edinburgh's
famous 'Resting Giant' with an
exploration of the local folklore and
customs associated with the mountain-
within-a-city.

Inspired by NVA's Speed of Light,
a major event in Edinburgh's
International Festival and the country-
wide Cultural Olympiad, *Journeys
and Evocations* brings together past
and future in a perspective of the
Edinburgh landscape like no other.

Details of these and other books published by Luath Press can be found at:
www.luath.co.uk

Luath Press Limited
committed to publishing well written books worth reading

LUATH PRESS takes its name from Robert Burns, whose little collie Luath (*Gael.*, swift or nimble) tripped up Jean Armour at a wedding and gave him the chance to speak to the woman who was to be his wife and the abiding love of his life. Burns called one of 'The Twa Dogs' Luath after Cuchullin's hunting dog in Ossian's *Fingal*. Luath Press was established in 1981 in the heart of Burns country, and now resides a few steps up the road from Burns' first lodgings on Edinburgh's Royal Mile. Luath offers you distinctive writing with a hint of unexpected pleasures.

Most bookshops in the UK, the US, Canada, Australia, New Zealand and parts of Europe either carry our books in stock or can order them for you. To order direct from us, please send a £sterling cheque, postal order, international money order or your credit card details (number, address of cardholder and expiry date) to us at the address below. Please add post and packing as follows: UK – £1.00 per delivery address; overseas surface mail – £2.50 per delivery address; overseas airmail – £3.50 for the first book to each delivery address, plus £1.00 for each additional book by airmail to the same address. If your order is a gift, we will happily enclose your card or message at no extra charge.

Luath Press Limited
543/2 Castlehill
The Royal Mile
Edinburgh EH1 2ND
Scotland

Telephone: 0131 225 4326 (24 hours)
email: sales@luath.co.uk
Website: www.luath.co.uk